JEWELS

FOR THE

SOUL

*Spiritual Reflections
and Affirmations
for the
Heart and Soul*

By
Kathryn Peters-Brinkley

HeartLight Productions

HeartLight Productions
1000 N. Green Valley Pkwy. Suite 440-292
Henderson, NV 89074-6170

First Quality Paperback Edition 1993
Originally entitled Love is my Only Master
Copyright © 1993, Kathryn M. Peters

Second Edition 2004
Jewels for the Soul
Copyright © 2004, Kathryn Peters-Brinkley

Cover and text design by Peggy Fuller

10 9 8 7 6 5 4 3 2 1

ISBN 0-9638490-1-8

Printed and bound in the United States of America

Dedication

My Sweet Mother,

I dedicate this book to you. God *filled* me with the spirit of Love, but only you taught me *how* to Love.
Thanks, Mom.

Acknowledgments

To Uriel and Mylonka, as your channel I have found my peace and my purpose.

I want to extend my heartfelt appreciation to my family for enduring my endless preoccupation during the gestation of this project. And I thank them each for choosing to be a part of my life and for the lessons they have volunteered to help me learn.

Dannion
You are the love of my life and the most sparkling jewel in my universe.

Elizabeth Michelle
By watching you step so gracefully into your magnificence, you gave me the courage to believe in myself.

Alixandra Dorian
You are a wonder! You have inspired me to never stop reaching for the unreachable.

Evan Jameson
Your shining eyes, beautiful smile and kind heart create a magic that has changed my life forever.

Alysia Kathryn
You are an exquisite combination of joy and fire. I am so glad we share a birthday, a name and a lifetime of love.

Angelica Arielle
The incredible beauty of your being is proof positive that angels do indeed live among us.

Adriana Nicholette
You have fortified my soul by your presence, and blessed me with another opportunity to love.

James Robert
Good friends are hard to find, but you have always remained one of my best. Thanks

INTRODUCTION

In 1975, I was struck by lightning. For two years afterwards, I struggled to recover. I could not walk, so I had to spend every painful day and sleepless night in my bed. Broken hearted, and desperate to be of help, my family and friends would bring me all kinds of books and magazines to read. I enjoyed the scientific and medical periodicals the most until the day I discovered a booklet called, The Upper Room, *in my stack.* The Upper Room *was filled with lots of short stories and inspiring parables about life's journey from tragedy to triumph. Each story had a reflection or affirmation at the end of it to help the reader derive the maximum benefit. I soon found myself wanting to read more and more of this kind of inspirational material in order to keep myself motivated as I recovered from my debilitating condition. On more than one occasion, I can remember feeling that those words of divine inspiration had literally saved my life.*

In 1994, my first book, Saved By The Light was published. It was a literary success, and as a result, I was asked to do hundreds of interviews, for newspapers and magazines. After doing a couple hundred of these, it got quite tedious. But one day, I picked up the telephone to do yet another one, and I heard the voice of an angel on the other end. Kathryn conducted a delightful interview that left me wanting to talk to her some more.

As we were saying good-bye, she offered to send me her book of reflections and affirmations. I readily accepted. When I received the book, I sat down eagerly, to peruse it. I found it to be spiritually comforting, and highly thought provoking. Of all the books of this genre, **Jewels For The Soul** *is one of the very best.*

I recommend that you start each day by opening this book to wherever you are guided. Your life will truly be blessed and enriched by the reflections and affirmations found within these pages.

Dannion Brinkley
September 17, 2004

How To Use This Book

As the flaming sun dawns each morning, life deserves to be celebrated anew. By avowing to consciously focus our thoughts and actions on the qualities of Spirit, we show reverence for the life within and surrounding us. **Jewels for the Soul** are to be planted in your mind and heart each morning as you begin your day, and again each evening, as your day draws to an end. If this is done with sincerity and regularity, these jewels will assist you in affirming the loving presence of Spirit in your soul and the awesome workings of Spirit in your life.

Jewels for the Soul may be meditated upon in order, as they appear in the book, or you may use your intuition to find the jewel best suited to your needs at any particular moment. This is done by silently embracing a thought or question. Then, simply allow the book to open naturally. The page your eyes falls upon first, will offer you either the guidance you are seeking, or the wisdom that you have forgotten.

Dear friends, I offer these spiritual reflections and affirmations to you as jewels of motivation and inspiration. Thoughts are power. The thoughts we hold dearest will manifest in our lives, without fail, for better or worse. So allow yourself the pleasure of beautiful thoughts. As you turn the pages of this book, open your heart to the Voice of Spirit, and open your life to the Miracle of Love.

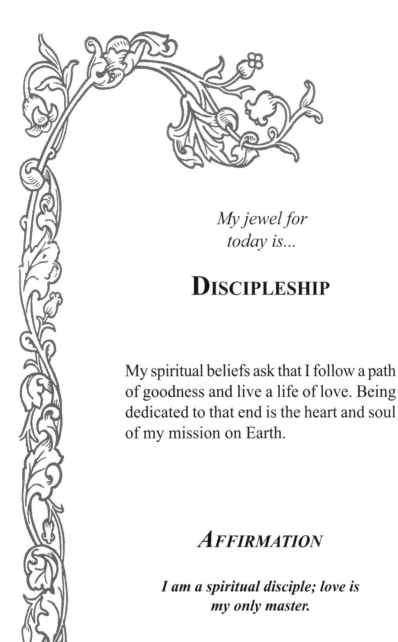

*My jewel for
today is...*

DISCIPLESHIP

My spiritual beliefs ask that I follow a path
of goodness and live a life of love. Being
dedicated to that end is the heart and soul
of my mission on Earth.

AFFIRMATION

***I am a spiritual disciple; love is
my only master.***

Jewels for the Soul

1

*My jewel for
today is...*

My Spiritual Self-Portrait

If placed before a blank canvas and asked to create
my self-portrait, how would I look? Would I draw
my eyes too small or too large, or would I see and
convey the shining light of Spirit behind them?
As I consider the way in which I see myself, first
I must view my eternal self through the unerring
eyes of Mother Goddess.

Affirmation

***As only a mother can, the Goddess has seen my
perfection from the beginning of time.***

Jewels for the Soul

2

*My jewel for
today is...*

HIGHER CONSCIOUSNESS

It has been said, that if I knock, the door will be
opened. Today, I will knock upon the door of
Higher Mind, for I wish to think the thoughts
of Spirit. And I shall knock once more, for I
yearn to know the peace of God.

AFFIRMATION

**The entrance to Higher Consciousness shall be
made visible when I approach it with a
sincere heart and an open mind.**

Jewels for the Soul

*My jewel for
today is...*

PRAYER

There have been times in my life when I could neither reach clarity or serenity of being, no matter how often I meditated, nor how hard I tried. It is in these times of isolation that I must ask for the Vision of Heaven. In other words, I must pray.

AFFIRMATION

Through heartfelt prayer I give the Holy Spirit permission to cleanse my heart, clear my mind, and heal my spirit.

Jewels for the Soul

4

*My jewel for
today is...*

LOVING SERVITUDE

Through every act of loving kindness and every word of encouragement I give to my fellow souls of Light, I am acting in loving servitude to Almighty Spirit. Above all else, I have come to Earth to be of service to the Family of God.

AFFIRMATION

***Each day and in every moment, I vow to
lovingly serve the one and only Great
Spirit of Love.***

Jewels for the Soul

*My jewel for
today is...*

·THE SIGNIFICANCE OF LIFE

I am not upon this Earth simply to dream of and strive for the day, out yonder, when my soul is finally freed from the physical realm. Life is a magical journey in and of itself. It is a quest for love, discovery, and celebration. If it is life eternal that I seek, let me step into eternity today.

AFFIRMATION

**The true significance of life is found in the
very moment I am living.**

Jewels for the Soul

*My jewel for
today is...*

DISCERNING ANGELS

My angels are the Guardians of my Light in this realm of shadow. Angels are present to instill hope, respond to prayer and affirmation, along with overseeing my progress upon the Emerald Sphere. Acknowledging the presence and power of angels in my life is the first step I will take toward establishing a lifelong love affair with miracles.

AFFIRMATION

*My dear Angels of Mercy, I call upon you this day
to assist me in discerning your presence
and accepting your help.*

Jewels for the Soul

*My jewel for
today is...*

Right Mindfulness

In a single day, I am bombarded from all directions by rumors of war and tales of humanity's inhumanity. In addition, my personal world is filled with endless demands to meet, as well as, countless responsibilities to shoulder. In order to successfully maneuver my way through all of this, to the peace of God, I must maintain right mindfulness.

Affirmation

When I can recognize the presence and power of Divinity in each and every life experience, I am successfully maintaining right mindfulness.

Jewels for the Soul

My jewel for
today is...

THE VIRTUE OF PATIENCE

Once I become cognizant of the creative power given to me by the presence of the Indwelling Christ, I need also become cognizant of the Divine mandate for patience. I create my own reality, yet the manifestation of that reality is not always according to my personal timing. The Universe oversees my life and delivers my highest good in a moment of perfection.

AFFIRMATION

By manifesting the virtue of patience, I cultivate
my faith in the perfection of the Universe.

Jewels for the Soul

*My jewel for
today is...*

Looking Beyond Appearances

Within my daily life, often, unsettling situations arise that leave me feeling disturbed or resentful. When this happens, it is to my best advantage if I can train myself to look beyond the appearance of injustice, inconvenience, or disagreement. With a little practice I will begin to see that just under the surface of every apparent adversity lies the seed of my future joy.

Affirmation

***It is only my judgment of a situation that blinds me
from seeing the endless good that lies just
beyond its appearance.***

Jewels for the Soul

*My jewel for
today is...*

FLOWING WITH SPIRIT

Life on Earth is a material projection of Spirit's holy imagination. The cosmic stream of consciousness flows on course, ever steady, ever strong. As an individuation of Spirit, I am one with the flow of life. I am inseparable from the flow of Spirit.

AFFIRMATION

My soul recognizes only tranquility and my heart experiences only love when I am aligned with the flow of Spirit.

Jewels for the Soul

*My jewel for
today is...*

TAPPING INTO PAST LIVES

All that I am this moment, is the culmination of all that I have been over the course of many lifetimes. Understanding my past assists me in making the most of my present. Moreover, the key to my future may well be awaiting me in an ancient memory stored in my eternal soul.

AFFIRMATION

**Tapping into past lives enables me to make
tremendous strides upon the path of
self-understanding and spiritual unfoldment.**

Jewels for the Soul

*My jewel for
today is...*

FINDING MY PURPOSE

Why am I here? What is it that I have to offer the world? How many times I have asked these questions, fully expecting the voice of Heaven to answer me? Yet, the answers are so obvious, if only I have eyes to see! What am I good at? What is it that I really enjoy doing that also brings joy to others? Once I have answered these questions, I will know, without a doubt, why I am here.

AFFIRMATION

***To find my purpose, I need look no further than
the desires of my heart.***

Jewels for the Soul

*My jewel for
today is...*

INNER WISDOM

The information and knowledge needed to help me successfully champion my life cannot be ascertained through external sources. Without fail, on a daily basis, I need to turn Inward. I need to enter the silence of holy reverence. Within the silence, I will receive the inner wisdom that is available to me and can only be transmitted through the Indwelling Christ.

AFFIRMATION

**My inner wisdom speaks in the language
of Infinite Love.**

Jewels for the Soul

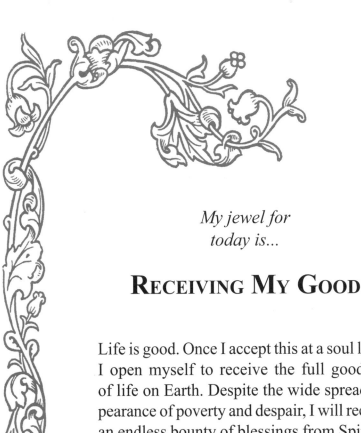

*My jewel for
today is...*

RECEIVING MY GOOD

Life is good. Once I accept this at a soul level,
I open myself to receive the full goodness
of life on Earth. Despite the wide spread appearance of poverty and despair, I will receive
an endless bounty of blessings from Spirit, if
it is here that I keep my mind focused.

AFFIRMATION

**As a Child of Divinity, I am entitled to receive
only the best of everything in my life.**

Jewels for the Soul

15

*My jewel for
today is...*

REMAINING CORRECT

As I am learning to allow myself to be swept uphill
by the increases of life's unending flow, I need also
pay attention to the way in which I conduct myself
in times of inevitable decrease. In remaining
correct, I am asked by the Universe to act as a
noble champion of spiritual ideals, regardless of
any challenges facing me.

AFFIRMATION

***I am a Spiritual Warrior dedicated to remaining
correct to all Divine Principles.***

Jewels for the Soul

*My jewel for
today is...*

ASTROLOGY

Over two millennia ago, the ancient astrologers foretold the coming of the Prince of Peace by looking into the face of Heaven and interpreting Her signs. This art remains as valid and as invaluable a tool for self-discovery today as it was to the seers and prophets of antiquity. A sincere desire to learn the basics of astrology will serve to accelerate my spiritual self-unfoldment.

AFFIRMATION

When I look to the stars, I behold the many faces of God.

Jewels for the Soul

17

*My jewel for
today is...*

TRANSFORMATION

As a worker of light, I have come to planet Earth to
offer my assistance to the salvation of this beauteous
orb and Her children. Along the way, I have
chosen to learn a few personal lessons as well. As I
habitually keep my mind on Spirit, regardless of the
circumstances challenging me to grow, I transcend
the Earth's consciousness. Thusly, I facilitate the
transformation of the human vibration.

AFFIRMATION

**A transformation of my thinking
transforms the world.**

Jewels for the Soul

*My jewel for
today is...*

BELIEVING IN MAGIC

To truly be alive is to be open to the real magic that exists within my soul. Magic surrounds me like the warmth of a mother's embrace. The magic in giving and receiving love fills me with unlimited potential. The magic of believing in myself turns that potential into the reality of my true being.

AFFIRMATION

When I learn to believe in magic, the gates of Heaven open wide and shower my life with enchantment from the inside out.

Jewels for the Soul

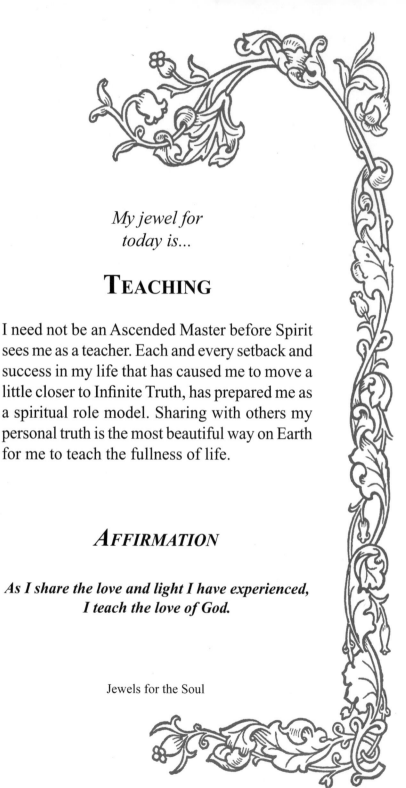

*My jewel for
today is...*

TEACHING

I need not be an Ascended Master before Spirit sees me as a teacher. Each and every setback and success in my life that has caused me to move a little closer to Infinite Truth, has prepared me as a spiritual role model. Sharing with others my personal truth is the most beautiful way on Earth for me to teach the fullness of life.

AFFIRMATION

**As I share the love and light I have experienced,
I teach the love of God.**

Jewels for the Soul

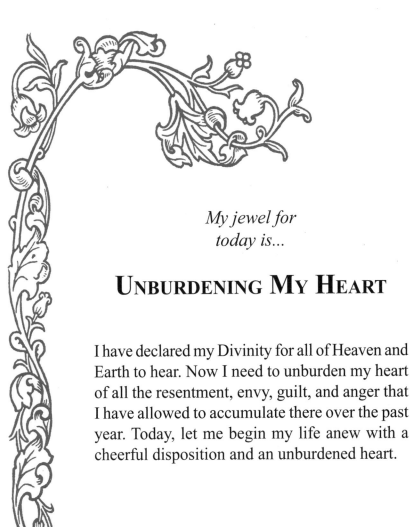

*My jewel for
today is...*

Unburdening My Heart

I have declared my Divinity for all of Heaven and Earth to hear. Now I need to unburden my heart of all the resentment, envy, guilt, and anger that I have allowed to accumulate there over the past year. Today, let me begin my life anew with a cheerful disposition and an unburdened heart.

Affirmation

***Divine Love will be magnetically drawn to my
heart when it has been emptied of all
hurt & malice.***

Jewels for the Soul

*My jewel for
today is...*

WALKING MY TALK

If I had time to digest the wisdom contained in every metaphysical volume ever written, not one word of it would benefit me, unless I could put those words of wisdom into practical, daily application. To be well read is to be nothing more than an educated fool without the ability to walk the talk.

AFFIRMATION

**Dear One, my heart fills with joy when
I know I am being faithful to
Your word.**

Jewels for the Soul

*My jewel for
today is...*

SAYING YES TO LIFE

Life asks that I grow. Life asks that I be happy.
Life asks that I procreate life. I need to answer
YES, YES, YES! I say yes to life as I continue
to study and learn the wonders of the universe.
I say yes to life as I choose to see the good
and the beautiful in everyone I meet and every
situation I encounter. I say yes to life when I
contribute a living act of love to the world.

AFFIRMATION

***With a smile, warm and genuine, on my lips,
with unquestioning love in my heart, and with
Spirit always on my mind, I say YES to life.***

Jewels for the Soul

*My jewel for
today is...*

BEAUTIFYING MY HOME

Because Spirit is beauty, I am Divinely led
to manifest the presence of this indwelling
loveliness. I can reveal the splendor of Spirit in
a myriad of ways, but in beautifying my home, I
bring great joy to Heaven. Whether my home is
great or small, in the heart of the Mother-Father
God, it is consecrated as sacred space by the
presence of the Living Spirit of Divine Beauty.

AFFIRMATION

*From this day forward I dedicate my home as a
Holy temple, devoted only to the nurturing
of spiritual love and beauty.*

Jewels for the Soul

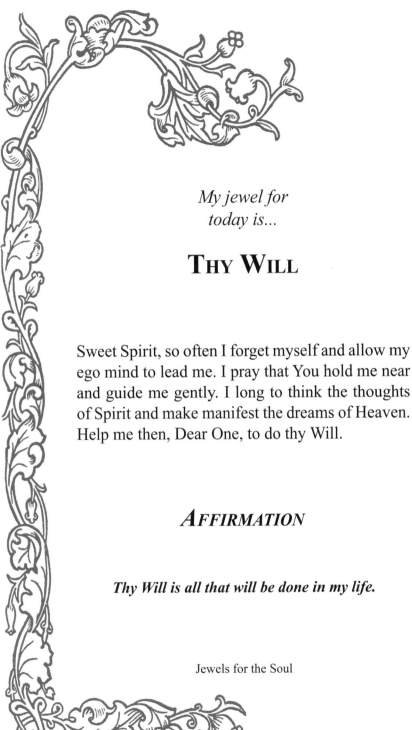

My jewel for
today is...

THY WILL

Sweet Spirit, so often I forget myself and allow my ego mind to lead me. I pray that You hold me near and guide me gently. I long to think the thoughts of Spirit and make manifest the dreams of Heaven. Help me then, Dear One, to do thy Will.

AFFIRMATION

Thy Will is all that will be done in my life.

Jewels for the Soul

*My jewel for
today is...*

IGNORING GOSSIP

Idle words produced by idle minds create only suffering. The spreading of embellished half-truths is no less than verbal and emotional abuse. I must never allow my being to become poisoned by the likes of this brand of treachery.

AFFIRMATION

**Sweet Spirit, from my mouth, let there flow
only words of kindness and truth.**

Jewels for the Soul

*My jewel for
today is...*

Psychic Self-Protection

It is mandatory, before journeying out into the world each day, that I automatically surround and protect myself with the White Light of Love. Enveloped by this impenetrable cosmic force field, I am shielded from every conceivable adversary of the Light.

Affirmation

**I am a Spiritual Warrior proudly donning
the shield of the Everliving One.**

Jewels for the Soul

*My jewel for
today is...*

CREATING MY REALITY

There is much talk being spread concerning the upcoming "Great Shift." More than a shift of the earth on its axis, I must concern myself with a personal and planetary shift in consciousness. For through my personal consciousness, my personal reality is created. Private thoughts of peace and love create a more peaceful, loving world.

AFFIRMATION

The state of my life reflects my state of mind.

Jewels for the Soul

*My jewel for
today is...*

FINANCIAL STABILITY

In the world of Spirit, truth will set my soul free. In the world of man, my physical freedom is attained through financial stability. It is my personal responsibility to see to it that I have sufficient finances to support my physical survival, my spiritual questing, and my loftiest of dreams. Souls who have no money for food, have little time to ponder the wonders of Spirit.

AFFIRMATION

Divine Oneness, as I free my mind from the struggle of finances, I free my hands and my heart to do Thy work.

Jewels for the Soul

29

*My jewel for
today is...*

EXPECT THE UNEXPECTED

Upon entering the physical realm, my soul understood that the life before me was designed to prepare me for mastership. The journey can take as long as I like. My key to success is learning to ready myself, in all ways and at all times, for the unexpected. Attempting to second guess the Universe will only serve to assure my frustration.

AFFIRMATION

***By expecting the unexpected, I surrender my soul to
the Infinite Wisdom of Spirit.***

Jewels for the Soul

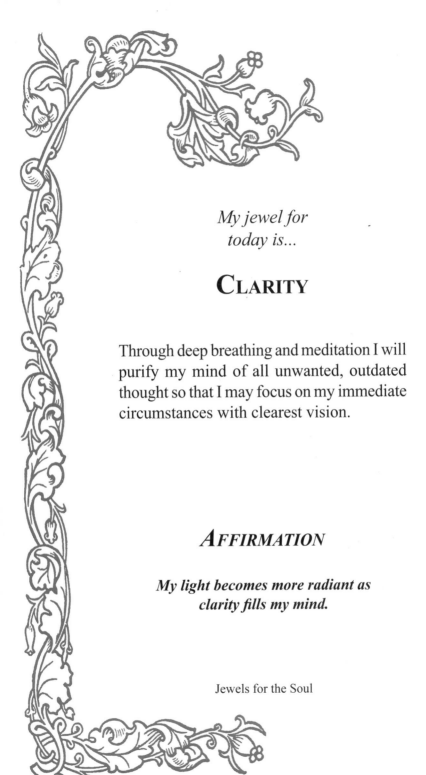

*My jewel for
today is...*

CLARITY

Through deep breathing and meditation I will
purify my mind of all unwanted, outdated
thought so that I may focus on my immediate
circumstances with clearest vision.

AFFIRMATION

**My light becomes more radiant as
clarity fills my mind.**

Jewels for the Soul

*My jewel for
today is...*

Pure Intent

Once my mind is clear, I can examine my personal
motivations honestly. As a Child of Light, I need
to contribute to the well being of my global family.
Therefore, I need to be conscious of how my heart
thoughts touch the lives of others.

Affirmation

**I will infuse this day with my purest intentions
for the highest good of all.**

Jewels for the Soul

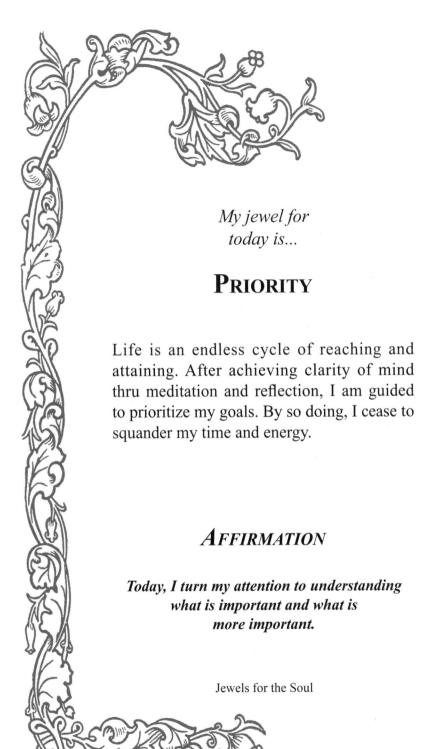

*My jewel for
today is...*

PRIORITY

Life is an endless cycle of reaching and attaining. After achieving clarity of mind thru meditation and reflection, I am guided to prioritize my goals. By so doing, I cease to squander my time and energy.

AFFIRMATION

**Today, I turn my attention to understanding
what is important and what is
more important.**

Jewels for the Soul

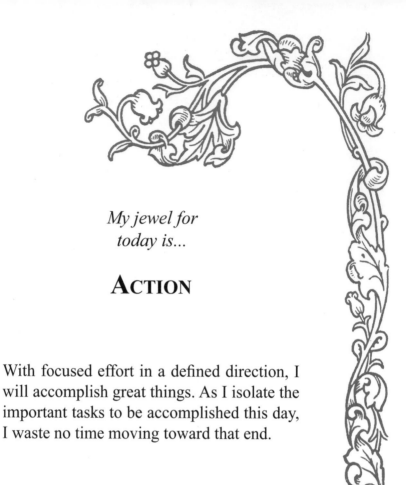

*My jewel for
today is...*

ACTION

With focused effort in a defined direction, I will accomplish great things. As I isolate the important tasks to be accomplished this day, I waste no time moving toward that end.

AFFIRMATION

Today, I will initiate positive action in the direction of my desired success.

Jewels for the Soul

*My jewel for
today is...*

FAITH

Knowing that physical or material manifestation
is not often immediate, I put my faith into practice
where tangible results seem to be lacking.

AFFIRMATION

**My will is my wand, therefore, I have faith
that all my goals will be reached in
the right and perfect time.**

Jewels for the Soul

*My jewel for
today is...*

PATIENCE

Spirit's perception of time and space differs vastly from my own. As a Child of Spirit, I need to respect the Infinite Wisdom of the All That Is and strive to develop the quality of patience.

AFFIRMATION

Every desire of my heart will come to me in the perfect timing of Divine Spirit.

Jewels for the Soul

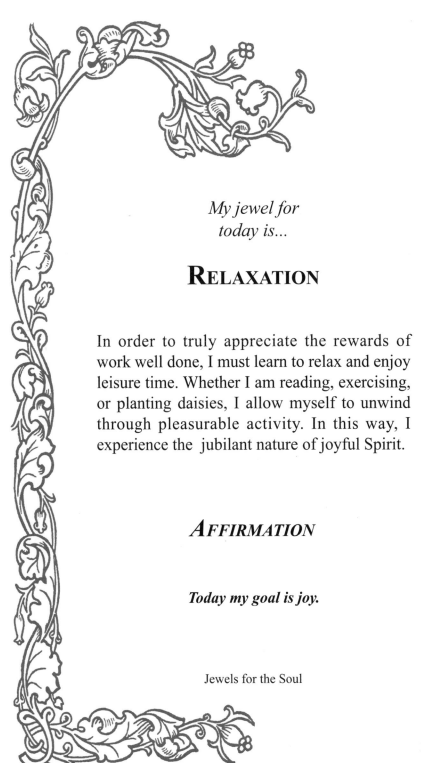

*My jewel for
today is...*

RELAXATION

In order to truly appreciate the rewards of work well done, I must learn to relax and enjoy leisure time. Whether I am reading, exercising, or planting daisies, I allow myself to unwind through pleasurable activity. In this way, I experience the jubilant nature of joyful Spirit.

AFFIRMATION

Today my goal is joy.

Jewels for the Soul

*My jewel for
today is...*

Body Appreciation

Standing unclothed before a full-length mirror, I admire my physical body. I now give bountiful thanks to my body for the countless ways it faithfully performs, on my behalf, each and every day.

Affirmation

I fill my body with love and gratitude.

Jewels for the Soul

*My jewel for
today is...*

COMMUNICATING MY LOVE

Following my sacred path means that I allow myself to be Spirit led in all that I do. Today, Spirit leads me to fill my being with love. Therefore, it leads me to communicate unconditional love through frequent acts of unselfishness and caring.

AFFIRMATION

*A heart full of love is an instrument of the
Holy Mother only when it is emptied
into the lives of others.*

Jewels for the Soul

*My jewel for
today is...*

SALUTING THE DIVINITY IN ALL

There is nothing in the Universe that brings more pain
to the Heart of God than the killing of her children in
the name of religion and righteousness. How can it
be that we believe God to be love, yet we spread such
hatred and horror in His name? I now avow to do all
that I can to spread the love and kindness of a gentle
God. I will begin by taking time this day, to salute the
Divinity in everyone I meet.

AFFIRMATION

***Holy Spirit, I honor You by saluting Your
Divine Presence in the heart of
everyone I meet.***

Jewels for the Soul

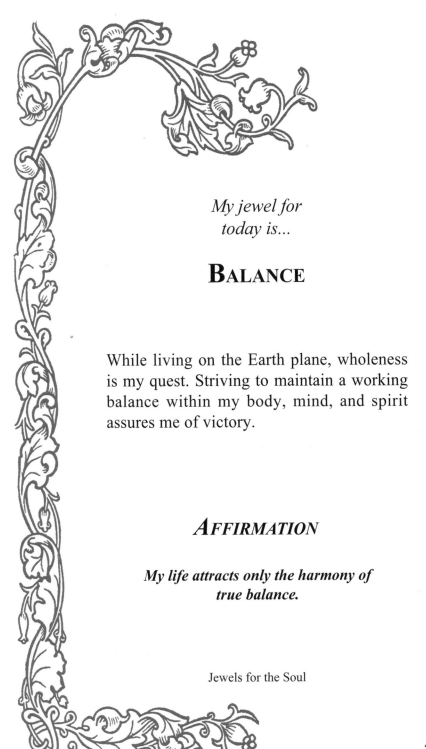

*My jewel for
today is...*

BALANCE

While living on the Earth plane, wholeness
is my quest. Striving to maintain a working
balance within my body, mind, and spirit
assures me of victory.

AFFIRMATION

**My life attracts only the harmony of
true balance.**

Jewels for the Soul

*My jewel for
today is...*

RIGHTEOUS INDIGNATION

The world has been forever changed by the invention of the television, the computer, and the digital magic of Hollywood. We have become so saturated with violence, atrocities, and horror shows, that little seems to shock us anymore. As a Child of Light, I cannot allow this mental numbing to overtake me. I must take a stand, in righteous indignation, against anything that is harmful to the human spirit.

AFFIRMATION

I am a torchbearer for the Light of Righteousness.

Jewels for the Soul

*My jewel for
today is...*

VOLUNTEERING TIME TO MY COMMUNITY

There is no mistake that I find myself a member of my community. Life has placed me where I need to be so that I might teach and learn through community interaction and involvement. When there is nothing more to give or receive where I am, life will move me elsewhere. In the meantime, I will help myself by helping others in my community.

AFFIRMATION

***A God-given talent becomes a gift of the greatest
value when it is shared with others.***

Jewels for the Soul

*My jewel for
today is...*

DESIGNING MY PRIVATE SANCTUARY

During times of contemplation and meditation, my experience of peace and serenity will be magnified if I place myself in a sanctuary of my own making. Into my sacred space I can bring my favorite spiritual objects, as well as, soothing smells, sounds, and colors that further enhance the mood of Divinity I wish to create.

AFFIRMATION

I will design a private sanctuary, which will recreate the beauteous serenity of my Indwelling Spirit.

Jewels for the Soul

*My jewel for
today is...*

A RESPLENDENT PRESENCE

Each day I display the luminance of the Light of Spirit within me by means of my physical appearance. As a child of Light, it is my duty to look and smell beautiful. The colors I choose, as well as the condition of the clothing I wear, all reflects my state of Spirit.

AFFIRMATION

***My physical appearance brings light and
beauty to the world.***

Jewels for the Soul

*My jewel for
today is...*

INTUITION

Many of my sensations and perceptions cannot be explained by logical means. I must learn to trust my spiritual insight and to depend upon my spontaneous knowing.

AFFIRMATION

**I will faithfully obey the small voice
within me.**

Jewels for the Soul

*My jewel for
today is...*

BROTHERHOOD

There is no man, woman, or child alive on Mother Earth this day who is not a unique and precious member of my global family.

AFFIRMATION

***I will recognize everyone I meet as a Divine
counter-part of myself.***

Jewels for the Soul

*My jewel for
today is...*

ACCEPTANCE

I cannot always control the circumstances of
my life. Nor am I always equipped to do so.
Tranquility is mine. For I know there is a Higher
Intelligence at work in all my affairs.

AFFIRMATION

In all ways, I will the Will of Spirit.

Jewels for the Soul

*My jewel for
today is...*

LOVING KINDNESS

Offering a cheery hello to a stranger or ex-
tending a helping hand to a soul in need are acts
of simple kindness which I must train myself to
perform automatically.

AFFIRMATION

**I am the heart of Spirit beating to
the rhythm of love.**

Jewels for the Soul

*My jewel for
today is...*

Non-Judgment

On the road to enlightenment, there are many beyond me. Many more are dragging their feet behind me. It is my personal progress that needs to occupy my thoughts.

Affirmation

Starting with myself, I will view every soul as a reflection of perfection.

Jewels for the Soul

*My jewel for
today is...*

HONORING MASCULINE ENERGY

Around the globe there are countless monuments honoring the genius and bravery of manhood. Of all the special tasks to be mastered through masculine energy, it is fatherhood that remains the most important and revered.

AFFIRMATION

**I salute and give thanks to the contributions
of the Universal masculine force.**

Jewels for the Soul

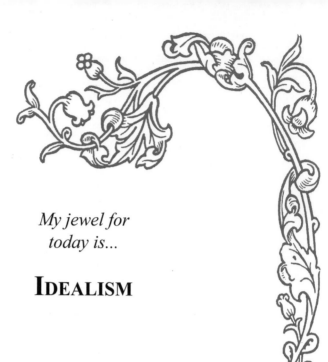

*My jewel for
today is...*

IDEALISM

Race consciousness is limiting. I will now allow my Higher Mind to do my thinking. I will allow myself to be infused with light. I will draw inspiration form the bosom of Spirit.

AFFIRMATION

I am propelled into genius by the mind of Spirit.

Jewels for the Soul

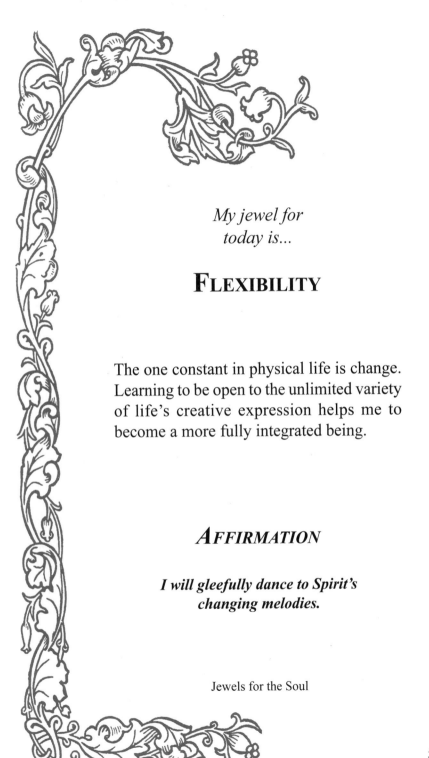

*My jewel for
today is...*

FLEXIBILITY

The one constant in physical life is change. Learning to be open to the unlimited variety of life's creative expression helps me to become a more fully integrated being.

AFFIRMATION

**I will gleefully dance to Spirit's
changing melodies.**

Jewels for the Soul

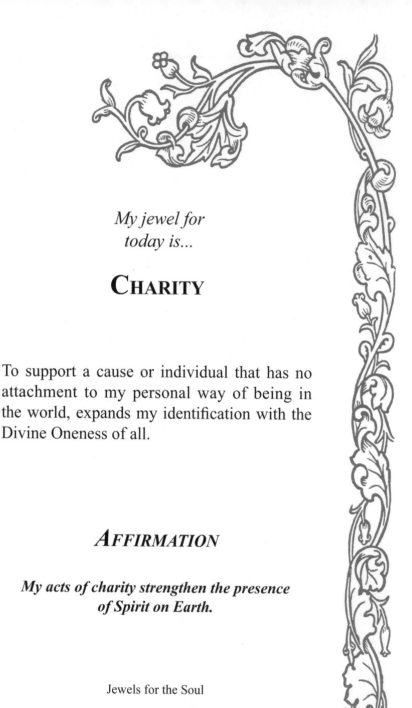

*My jewel for
today is...*

CHARITY

To support a cause or individual that has no
attachment to my personal way of being in
the world, expands my identification with the
Divine Oneness of all.

AFFIRMATION

**My acts of charity strengthen the presence
of Spirit on Earth.**

Jewels for the Soul

*My jewel for
today is...*

RELATIONSHIPS

Each of us enters and leaves the garden of life alone. Yet, without the gift of companionship, through family and friends, life's music falls on deaf ears.

AFFIRMATION

**I will consciously nurture all of my
relationships with tenderness.**

Jewels for the Soul

*My jewel for
today is...*

EMPOWERMENT

It is my responsibility in life to be my own most passionate advocate. I must defend myself from negativity and promote the flourishment of beauty in my sacred spaces.

AFFIRMATION

I am empowered by the Great I Am.

Jewels for the Soul

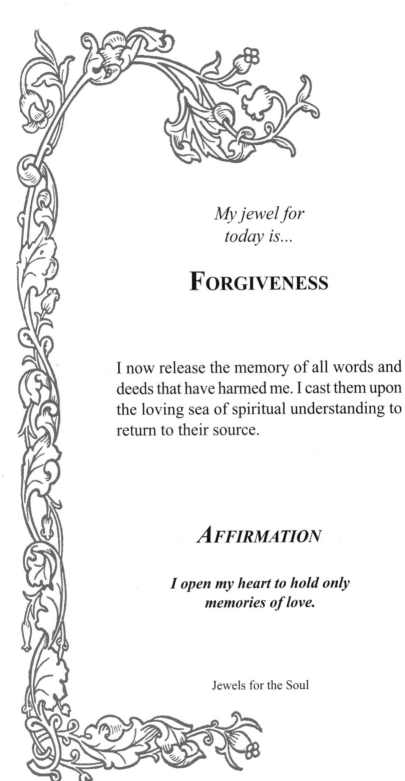

*My jewel for
today is...*

FORGIVENESS

I now release the memory of all words and deeds that have harmed me. I cast them upon the loving sea of spiritual understanding to return to their source.

AFFIRMATION

**I open my heart to hold only
memories of love.**

Jewels for the Soul

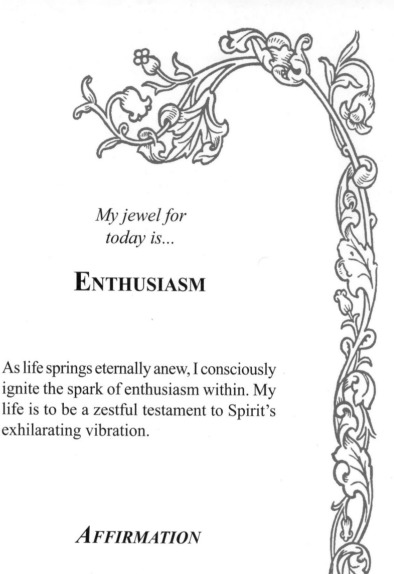

*My jewel for
today is...*

ENTHUSIASM

As life springs eternally anew, I consciously
ignite the spark of enthusiasm within. My
life is to be a zestful testament to Spirit's
exhilarating vibration.

AFFIRMATION

***I create each new day with enthusiasm
and excitement.***

Jewels for the Soul

*My jewel for
today is...*

DETACHED COMPASSION

Detached compassion is learning to care for the sick without coming down with the disease. I cannot allow the sorrows and disappointments of others to place obstacles upon my path.

AFFIRMATION

***I am not a beast of burden to carry others.
Instead, I aspire to be a torch to light their way.***

Jewels for the Soul

*My jewel for
today is...*

SELF-LOVE

Without vanity or conceit I am happy to be me. I am proud of who I am becoming and the spiritual lessons I have mastered.

AFFIRMATION

I am love.

Jewels for the Soul

*My jewel for
today is...*

CELEBRATION

Life is the most extraordinary collage of splendiferous events. Witnessing a sunrise, listening to the call of a mother robin, or bathing myself in the pale moonlight are all activities that beseech me to join the celebration of life.

AFFIRMATION

**I celebrate life and find joy in
every experience.**

Jewels for the Soul

*My jewel for
today is...*

SILENCE

Silence is the keeper of all mystery. I am infused with great strength and wisdom when I immerse myself in it's tranquility. On a daily basis, I can soothe my soul by taking the time to enter the sacred sanctuary of silence.

AFFIRMATION

**In the silence I learn to hear the
language of love.**

Jewels for the Soul

*My jewel for
today is...*

REPROGRAMMING

So much of what I do and say are leftovers from
the child or young adult I used to be. Today, I
am much wiser and more in touch with myself.
Therefore, I choose to reprogram myself from this
new perspective I have on life.

AFFIRMATION

*I live only in the now, and my reactions are based
on this present moment.*

Jewels for the Soul

*My jewel for
today is...*

NATIONAL PRIDE

I realize the many freedoms that bless my life
in this country. Yet, no nation on this globe has
reached political perfection. I stand proud to be
a member of this great country and I will help
Her, however I can, to heal Her wounds.

AFFIRMATION

**For all the positive energy my country has
generated on behalf of this world,
I am proud of Her.**

Jewels for the Soul

*My jewel for
today is...*

NEW EXPERIENCES

There are infinite opportunities awaiting me to experience something totally novel today. I could learn to skate, sign up for voice lessons, or plan a trip around the world. Wherever my interests lie, life is inviting me to live it to the fullest.

AFFIRMATION

I am open and willing to live life in a fresh and courageous manner.

Jewels for the Soul

*My jewel for
today is...*

CHOICE

As I entered this physical realm, I brought with me two things: my personal mission and free will. I am free to choose happiness, en-lightenment, and higher thought, no matter what circumstances challenge me this day.

AFFIRMATION

I protect and encourage my right to choose the best in myself, for myself, always.

Jewels for the Soul

*My jewel for
today is...*

THANKSGIVING

I am eternally grateful for the love and laughter that laces my life with joy. I am beholden to the friends and family who offer me acceptance. I am obliged to the situations that urge me to grow.

AFFIRMATION

I am thankful to Great Spirit for the showering of life's treasures, great and small.

Jewels for the Soul

*My jewel for
today is...*

DEMONSTRATION

There is a need in this world for a show of more love and light. In my personal world, I vow to demonstrate the love and tenderness of Spirit in very obvious and tangible ways.

AFFIRMATION

**I will express my love and spread my light
to all I encounter.**

Jewels for the Soul

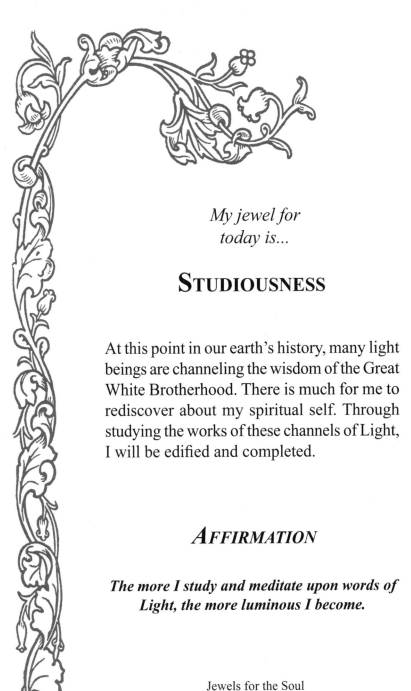

*My jewel for
today is...*

STUDIOUSNESS

At this point in our earth's history, many light beings are channeling the wisdom of the Great White Brotherhood. There is much for me to rediscover about my spiritual self. Through studying the works of these channels of Light, I will be edified and completed.

AFFIRMATION

The more I study and meditate upon words of Light, the more luminous I become.

Jewels for the Soul

*My jewel for
today is...*

DISCERNMENT

It has been said that truth will light upon my heart like the wings of an angel. So, it is feasible that I might overlook this gentle sign. Discernment is a quality of Spirit, when developed, that allows me to know when truth is spoken.

AFFIRMATION

I ask Spirit to bless me with the gift of discernment.

Jewels for the Soul

*My jewel for
today is...*

COMPANIONSHIP

So often, I tell friends that we must get together,
yet I do nothing to make that invitation a
reality. Today, I will reach out to a friend and
bring cheer into both our lives.

AFFIRMATION

**In the company of friends, I will find the
laughter and joy of Spirit.**

Jewels for the Soul

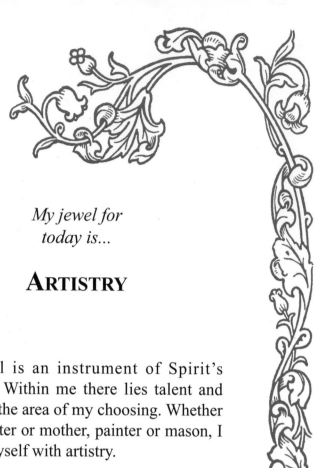

*My jewel for
today is...*

ARTISTRY

Each soul is an instrument of Spirit's creativity. Within me there lies talent and artistry in the area of my choosing. Whether I am a writer or mother, painter or mason, I express myself with artistry.

AFFIRMATION

**My personal artistry brings color and
imagination to my every task.**

Jewels for the Soul

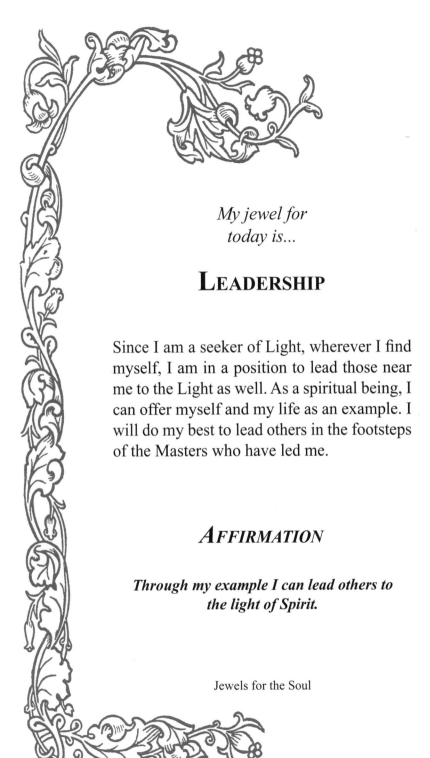

*My jewel for
today is...*

LEADERSHIP

Since I am a seeker of Light, wherever I find myself, I am in a position to lead those near me to the Light as well. As a spiritual being, I can offer myself and my life as an example. I will do my best to lead others in the footsteps of the Masters who have led me.

AFFIRMATION

**Through my example I can lead others to
the light of Spirit.**

Jewels for the Soul

73

*My jewel for
today is...*

PRAISE

Each of us on Earth, during these tumultuous times, is doing our best. All too often I forget to let my brothers and sisters know how much I appreciate their personal efforts to bring their uniqueness into our world.

AFFIRMATION

I will lift my voice in praise for every kindred soul in Spirit.

Jewels for the Soul

*My jewel for
today is...*

ABUNDANCE

In the eyes of Creative Spirit there is only abundance. Everything put upon this living planet was placed here lavishly. Abundance is my personal birthright.

AFFIRMATION

***It is the Will of Heaven, so I now open my
heart to receive lavish abundance
in all things.***

Jewels for the Soul

*My jewel for
today is...*

THOUGHTFULNESS

A note sent to cheer a loved one, a flower purchased to say I love you, or a dinner invitation for no special reason, are just a few of the things I can do to show those dear to me that I think of them with love.

AFFIRMATION

**Great Spirit, lead my heart to do your works
through thoughtfulness.**

Jewels for the Soul

*My jewel for
today is...*

GENTLE STRENGTH

The way of the TAO is the art of gentleness.
As a Spiritual Warrior, I show my greatest
strength when my sword is made of gentle
words and loving actions.

AFFIRMATION

**In all ways, let me penetrate the dark veil of
ignorance with gentleness.**

Jewels for the Soul

*My jewel for
today is...*

SPIRITUAL FLUENCY

Not everyone I meet recognizes the same spiritual alphabet. Our languages may differ, but our Source is the same. I must learn to be a spiritual linguist, speaking and hearing words that bring me ever closer to my human family.

AFFIRMATION

***I will speak from an open heart and I will allow
Spirit to be my loving interpreter.***

Jewels for the Soul

*My jewel for
today is...*

DAYDREAMING

There is nothing that has ever been accomplished that I cannot accomplish... and more. Learning to daydream again can strengthen my spirit, uplift my heart, and empower my daily efforts.

AFFIRMATION

**The fulfillment of all my dreams is part of
Spirit's divine plan.**

Jewels for the Soul

*My jewel for
today is...*

COMMUNION

As the pressures of the physical realm draw near to my sacred space, I discipline myself to automatically initiate communion with my Highest Self. In this practice, my spiritual balance need never be endangered.

AFFIRMATION

**I encircle myself with the Violet Ray, as I
spiritually commune with my
purest inbeing.**

Jewels for the Soul

*My jewel for
today is...*

EVOLUTION

I have studied, meditated, and affirmed my way
to a certain level of spiritual confidence. Yet,
the truth I seek is as infinite and dynamic as
my Loving Source.

AFFIRMATION

*I am poised, ready to receive any and all new
information which will facilitate my
soul's evolution.*

Jewels for the Soul

*My jewel for
today is...*

REINFORCING MY GOOD

The inequities and atrocities of this realm are boisterously broadcast from dawn to moonrise. To achieve my spiritual ends, I must constantly remind myself of all that is right and perfect in my world.

AFFIRMATION

As a spiritual being, my reality is love and light.

Jewels for the Soul

*My jewel for
today is...*

My Christhood

Within my soul there dwells the power and majesty of Infinite Spirit. I now call forth the purity of the Christed One within my to be born anew. In reverence to the Mother-Father God, and with sacred longing in my heart, I declare my Christhood. I Am the Way, the Truth and the Life.

AFFIRMATION

My ascension into the realm of Light commences the instant I proclaim my Christhood.

Jewels for the Soul

*My jewel for
today is...*

JUBILATION

As I begin this new day, I will visualize myself experiencing only joy and happiness. I will see myself breathing cheer and jubilation into everyone and everything I touch.

AFFIRMATION

**My life is a jubilant expression of my
Creator's perfection.**

Jewels for the Soul

*My jewel for
today is...*

SELFLESSNESS

As an emissary of the Great Spirit, I have come
to Mother Earth to serve Her and Her children
through my unique contribution. Teach me,
Great One, to become selfless in my giving and
steadfast in my efforts.

AFFIRMATION

***As I give of myself without thought of reward, I
am rewarded beyond measure.***

Jewels for the Soul

*My jewel for
today is...*

UNIVERSAL RHYTHM

There is a natural rhythm to the Universe. An underlying, ever so subtle, musical theme to which life dances. Once I attune myself to the rhythm of the cosmos, my life will flow to the beat of perfection.

AFFIRMATION

I will choreograph my life to the music of the Celestial Composer.

Jewels for the Soul

*My jewel for
today is...*

SINGLE VISION

When my energies are scattered it is difficult for me to influence my world with real power. As I narrow my vision and streamline my field of purpose, I am more likely to impact others and accomplish great things.

AFFIRMATION

***As I train my eyes to have single vision, my true
abilities come into focus.***

Jewels for the Soul

*My jewel for
today is...*

THE PURGING OF DARKNESS

With the turning of the century, our Earth entered a time of gestation and rebirth. Humankind is being purged of its ignorance and insanity. Darkness may appear to prevail, but I will take heart in the bleakest hours. I know that Spirit is cleansing the human psyche in preparation for the dawning of the coming Age of Peace.

AFFIRMATION

***I will rise above the appearance of tragedy
and darkest disaster by holding firmly to Holy
Spirit's Wings of Love.***

Jewels for the Soul

*My jewel for
today is...*

SPIRITUAL MATURITY

No longer am I a babe in the Universe. I have been here, in one fashion or another since time immemorial. I now am cognizant of my responsibility to my Universal family and I vow to spread the Light of Spirit wherever I may travel.

AFFIRMATION

***As the human condition appears to be
regressing, Mother Earth requests
my spiritual maturity.***

Jewels for the Soul

*My jewel for
today is...*

STAMINA

The workload of the Spiritual Warrior is exhausting.
There are few thanks and long hours. Yet, the battle
for enlightenment cannot be abandoned. I play a
vital role in the salvation of my brotherhood.

AFFIRMATION

**Give me stamina, Dear One, and lead me
to Thy victory.**

Jewels for the Soul

*My jewel for
today is...*

Singing Spirit's Praises

Like a wilted flower, I can be rejuvenated by the nourishing words of encouragement and praise of a kindred spirit. In the same way, the infinite energy of the Great Spirit is magnified by my words of loving praise and appreciation.

Affirmation

**In all things, let me praise the
magnificence of Spirit.**

Jewels for the Soul

*My jewel for
today is...*

RELINQUISHING MY BELIEF IN DUALITY

If I so choose, I have the free will to concentrate my attention on that which is troubling, dark, and hateful in life. Or, I can choose to keep my mind focused on all things beautiful and loving. Belief in duality is learned behavior. It is a conditioned response to physical reality. Duality does not exist in the mind of God, therefore, it does not exist.

AFFIRMATION

In all that I embrace in life, there is only good, for God is Good, and Good is All That Is.

Jewels for the Soul

*My jewel for
today is...*

INDIVIDUAL OPINION

The One Light of Christ Consciousness manifests as millions of seemingly individual shining rays. Yet, each singular beam of light is but a reflection of the Original Source. For those traveling the lighted path, the opinions of others are to be regarded respectfully as individual reflections of Universal Truth.

AFFIRMATION

I will respect the individual opinions of my Earthly companions, for I understand the One Light can be reflected in a multitude of ways.

Jewels for the Soul

*My jewel for
today is...*

HONORING HARD WORK

To labor in the name of Spirit is indeed an honor in and of itself. It may appear that I work for money, yet in truth, I toil for the Love of Heaven. Whatever task busies my hands and mind each day is truly part of my Divine mission.

AFFIRMATION

**Until the pure Light of Heaven shines in the heart
of all humankind, I am dedicated to hard
work on Spirit's behalf.**

Jewels for the Soul

ORGANIZATION

The Infinite Universe is organized with a place
for everything and everything in its place. In my
personal universe I seek to emulate this Divine
order. Organizing my thoughts, my time, and my
home will increase my spiritual authenticity as
I release myself from the enervation of living
in the midst of clutter.

AFFIRMATION

**Infinite Mind, please bless my efforts to express
Divine Order in my daily life.**

Jewels for the Soul

*My jewel for
today is...*

PRODUCTIVITY

It is not enough that I go through the motions of
my life. Today I long to feel truly productive. To
be productive does not mean that I must do more.
It means that I must strive to be more and to share
more of myself, for the upliftment of others.

AFFIRMATION

**Holy Spirit, I ask to be your unfettered vessel so
that I may produce the kind of spiritual results
that make life on Earth more meaningful.**

Jewels for the Soul

*My jewel for
today is...*

PAYING ATTENTION TO DETAIL

The Cosmic Powers are constantly feeding me vital information from every direction. Yet, I often miss these important messages because I am not paying attention to detail. In my ignorance, I've dismissed the words of strangers and chalked up destiny to coincidence. By doing this, I have overlooked the obvious signs and signals from Spirit.

AFFIRMATION

I witness the presence of Spirit in every aspect of life when I learn to pay attention to detail.

Jewels for the Soul

97

*My jewel for
today is...*

BODY LANGUAGE

The way I hold my head, move my eyes, and carry my body all affect my personal vibration and the way I feel within my being.

AFFIRMATION

**In all circumstances, out of self-love, I project
the refinement of my Divine Nature.**

Jewels for the Soul

*My jewel for
today is...*

CONTACTING MY HIGHEST SELF

I am a multidimensional being. Simultaneously, I exist on all levels of consciousness. My Higher Self, that eternal part of me closest to the Holy Spirit, is always just a breath away. I can call on my Higher Self at any time for the wisdom and love I need.

AFFIRMATION

My Highest Self stands ready to lift me up in consciousness whenever I am ready to ask.

Jewels for the Soul

*My jewel for
today is...*

TREASURING CHILDREN

Every child I meet is a reflection of the vibrant
energy, Divine purity, and boundless love
emanating from Original Source. Children
are most blessed. They are the closest thing to
perfection on earth. To cherish and protect the
children is a Divine act of spiritual understanding.
For in this act we display appreciation for our
greatest global treasure.

AFFIRMATION

***Holy One, please bless me with a heart that
reaches out in love to all children.***

Jewels for the Soul

*My jewel for
today is...*

SPIRIT IN FORM

To understand my eternal identity is to understand
that I am Spirit in form. Spirit is the power that
animates my life. The breath of my being is the
life force of Divinity. To grasp this fact is to
unveil a great mystery.

AFFIRMATION

***While expressing myself as a physical being, I
am manifesting as Spirit in form.***

Jewels for the Soul

*My jewel for
today is...*

SELF-REALIZATION

As a spiritual being inhabiting a physical body,
I sometimes forget my eternal reality. In truth,
I am one with Spirit. I am boundless love. I am
endless light.

AFFIRMATION

*I must constantly remind myself of my spiritual
identity, for self-realization is my key to finding
my power and purpose on Earth.*

Jewels for the Soul

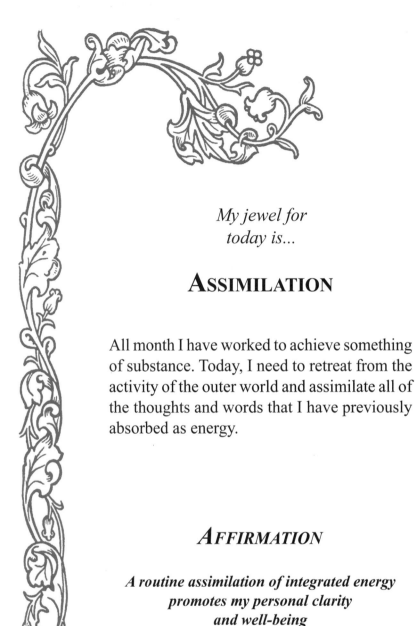

*My jewel for
today is...*

ASSIMILATION

All month I have worked to achieve something
of substance. Today, I need to retreat from the
activity of the outer world and assimilate all of
the thoughts and words that I have previously
absorbed as energy.

AFFIRMATION

*A routine assimilation of integrated energy
promotes my personal clarity
and well-being*

Jewels for the Soul

*My jewel for
today is...*

CHEERFUL SEPARATION

In every life there comes a time when two souls who have shared so much, come to a fork in their road. This may be so for lovers, business partners, good friends, or family members. No matter who is involved, separating paths can be quite painful to endure. Yet, in Sprit, two that have come together in the presence of love, shall be connected in love forevermore.

AFFIRMATION

***By co-operating with a cheerful separation, I free
us both to honor our sacred pathways.***

Jewels for the Soul

*My jewel for
today is...*

HARMONIZING MY ENVIRONMENT

The places and spaces in which I spend the majority of my time will actually contribute to my physical and spiritual well-being, if their energy harmonizes with my own. Proper lighting and color combine to elevate my mood and quicken my spirit.

AFFIRMATION

***For love of self, I need to harmonize my environment
with the vibration of my true inner essence.***

Jewels for the Soul

*My jewel for
today is...*

KNOWINGNESS

I cannot rely on the appearance of the present as a means of predicting the future. When I know in my heart, unwaveringly, where I want to go and what I want to achieve, there are no challenges upon my path that can stop me.

AFFIRMATION

***My knowingness tells me that my dreams were
first dreamed for me, by Spirit.***

Jewels for the Soul

*My jewel for
today is...*

SURRENDER

So often I wrangle with Spirit over the terms
of life in the physical realm. I want the human
condition to conform to my internal pictures
instead of accepting its present level of
evolution. I recurrently find myself resisting
the natural rhythms of the Earth dance.

AFFIRMATION

*I must sagaciously surrender to the dance of life
by allowing Spirit to set the tempo
and take the lead.*

Jewels for the Soul

*My jewel for
today is...*

GOOD CHEER

Several times in the New Testament the Christed One instructs us to be of good cheer. Being of good cheer is more than the mere practice of positive thinking. Good cheer is the mystical means by which we bring about constructive change in our lives. On the bleakest of occasions, a light touch or a contagious giggle can work true magic. In the darkest of times, my indwelling spirit can dance with glee to the melody of good cheer.

AFFIRMATION

I cast the bright light of hope when I call upon the spirit of good cheer.

Jewels for the Soul

*My jewel for
today is...*

EMOTIONAL MASTERY

As a Spiritual Warrior, it is paramount that I am master of my emotions. In order to carry out the intricate details of my earth assignment, I must have unyielding control over my thoughts, words, and deeds.

AFFIRMATION

**I am master of my fate when I am master
of my emotions.**

Jewels for the Soul

*My jewel for
today is...*

KEEPING A JOURNAL

My personal journey toward wholeness has taken me down many back roads and up just as many mountain trails. By recording daily entries into a spiritual journal, I intensify my cognitive process and accelerate my spiritual evolution.

AFFIRMATION

***A personal journal helps to keep me on course as
I tread the path to enlightenment.***

My jewel for
today is...

THE POWER OF PEACE

When I sustain only thoughts of love, I open myself to the experience of peace beyond measure. My day may be decorated in an eclectic showcase of people and circumstances that either help to focus or distract me. Yet, my daily mission is to bring the peace of Spirit into every situation I encounter.

AFFIRMATION

Connecting my mind with the Divine Mind
guarantees me the power of peace.

Jewels for the Soul

*My jewel for
today is...*

QUALITY OF LIFE

The living of my life is like the crafting of an exquisite piece of jewelry. First I must decide if I want the foundation of my life to be laid in gold or silver. Then I must carefully choose the gems that will reflect my luminance. The quality of my materials and the degree of my craftsmanship will determine, long after I am gone, whether or not this lifetime held true value.

AFFIRMATION

Crafting a quality life is my gift to Spirit.

Jewels for the Soul

*My jewel for
today is...*

TRUST

As the world prepares for the Age of Peace, it appears that we are being subjected to a reign of war and terror, Darkness seems to be gaining in strength. More mar-riages are ending in divorce, and more children are going to bed without food. But, in truth, Spirit is beckoning all darkness to come into the light so that it can be exposed, and vanquished. What is and what appears to be are not always the same. By trusting in the perfection of Spirit's divine plan, I will be able to see through the illusion of darkness.

AFFIRMATION

I trust my soul to see the Light of Spirit where my physical eyes can see naught.

Jewels for the Soul

*My jewel for
today is...*

VIGILANCE

So often I am tempted to allow my humanness
the first response to life. Living from within the
Light of Spirit, often requires more concentrated
effort on my part.

AFFIRMATION

**I am vigilant in my mission as a torchbearer
of Spirit's Living Light.**

Jewels for the Soul

*My jewel for
today is...*

LIVING IN THE NOW

By longing for days gone by or striving for times yet to come, I rob myself of the joy inherent in every present experience. Now is the only time I have to be happy. I must embrace each day as if it were the only one I will ever have.

AFFIRMATION

***Living in the now increases my ability to
experience and share the joy of Spirit.***

Jewels for the Soul

*My jewel for
today is...*

WHOLESOMENESS

To be a whole, self-actualized, and contributing member of humanity, I need to do all I can to increase my spiritual frequency. I achieve this end as I seek to emulate the wholesome nature of Spirit.

AFFIRMATION

**May the Divine Mind fill my soul with the
innocence and purity of Its wholesomeness.**

Jewels for the Soul

*My jewel for
today is...*

SPIRITUAL GIFTS

The Holy Spirit has blessed me with abundant gifts and talents. It is part of my earth assignment to recognize, strengthen, and utilize these gifts to my highest potential, for the good of all.

AFFIRMATION

I devote the use of my divinely given gifts and talents to the upliftment of humankind.

Jewels for the Soul

*My jewel for
today is...*

DIVINE RECOGNITION

As I behold the Light of Spirit shining forth from within my being, I need to recognize that same light as existing within each and every soul who happens across my path.

AFFIRMATION

I recognize the Divine Light of love within each soul who touches my life.

Jewels for the Soul

My jewel for
today is...

SOOTHING SOUND

There is a cosmic sound, a celestial choir forever chanting a placid accompaniment to the pulse of my personal energy. Filling my life with beautiful, melodic music will help me to recall the rhythms of Heaven.

AFFIRMATION

With Spirit in my heart, I will compose a symphony of personal tranquility.

Jewels for the Soul

*My jewel for
today is...*

COMMITMENT

In order to successfully fulfill my soul's purpose, I need to be committed to calling forth the best and brightest from within myself. As I commit to my personal and spiritual integrity, I easily become more clearly who I was born to be.

AFFIRMATION

I now commit my soul to the fulfillment of every spiritual ideal.

Jewels for the Soul

*My jewel for
today is...*

ACTIVE LISTENING

I nurture myself as I nurture my Earth family. When
I am actively listening to the feelings and thoughts
of those I know and love, I am nurturing a divine
aspect within both of us.

AFFIRMATION

**By listening to the heart of humankind, I will surely
hear the Voice of Spirit.**

Jewels for the Soul

*My jewel for
today is...*

CERTAINTY

All about me there are tragedies occurring in the lives of my global family. Even so, frustration and doubt cannot by granted admittance into my personal realm of thinking.

AFFIRMATION

With unshakable certainty, I place my life in the hands of Infinite Wisdom.

Jewels for the Soul

*My jewel for
today is...*

ROMANCE

My relationship to my Divine Source is romantic on the grandest scale. Spirit and I are one and the same. We are inseparable and bound eternally by love. Living in this spiritual harmony opens the door to manifesting romance in the physical.

AFFIRMATION

*I am made whole by giving and receiving the
Love of Spirit.*

Jewels for the Soul

*My jewel for
today is...*

SIMPLICITY

I can be truest to my spiritual path when I simplify my life and keep my eye single. Focusing on one task at a time allows me to keep myself in perfect balance.

AFFIRMATION

**As I simplify my life I magnify my
personal power.**

Jewels for the Soul

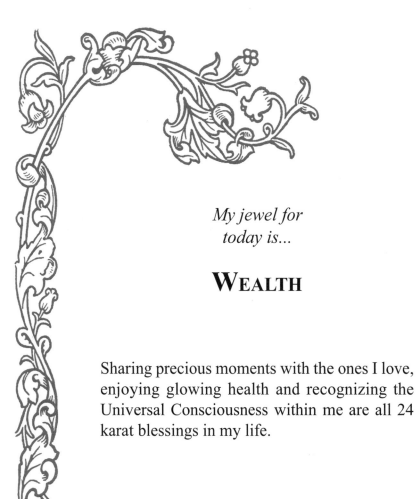

*My jewel for
today is...*

WEALTH

Sharing precious moments with the ones I love,
enjoying glowing health and recognizing the
Universal Consciousness within me are all 24
karat blessings in my life.

AFFIRMATION

**Through the gifts of Spirit, I find true and lasting
wealth.**

Jewels for the Soul

*My jewel for
today is...*

PARTNERSHIP

Many spiritual seekers have felt that, according to Cosmic Will, their lives simply unfold as necessary. Yet, the truth remains that Spirit and I are co-creators of my life. Together, we create all that I experience from moment to moment.

AFFIRMATION

***In partnership, Spirit and I collaborate to
create within my life something we both
can be proud of.***

Jewels for the Soul

*My jewel for
today is...*

OBEDIENCE

As I endeavor to attune myself to the frequency
of Spirit, it is not enough to simply pride myself
on hearing the small voice within. It is my duty
to also obey it.

AFFIRMATION

**My intuition is meaningless without
demonstrating obedience to the
Spirit who guides me.**

Jewels for the Soul

*My jewel for
today is...*

TIMING

In life, achievements, challenges, and blessings are all a matter of timing. After I have affirmed my desire and projected my gratitude and positivism into the Cosmos, I then need to rely on the perfection of Spirit's timing in the manifestation.

AFFIRMATION

**In the right and perfect time, all my dreams
shall be fulfilled.**

Jewels for the Soul

*My jewel for
today is...*

DIVINE OBSTACLES

From time to time I attract restrictions and limitations that cause me to feel that my spiritual progress is being hampered. In reality, every difficulty is Divinely planned to serve my highest good.

AFFIRMATION

***I behold a loving blessing in each Divine
obstacle I have chosen to experience.***

Jewels for the Soul

*My jewel for
today is...*

EVALUATION

At varying intervals in my life, it is beneficial for me to take stock of what I have absorbed and assimilated from my myriad of life occurrences.

AFFIRMATION

By evaluating my present status, I act to reset my course and empower my future.

Jewels for the Soul

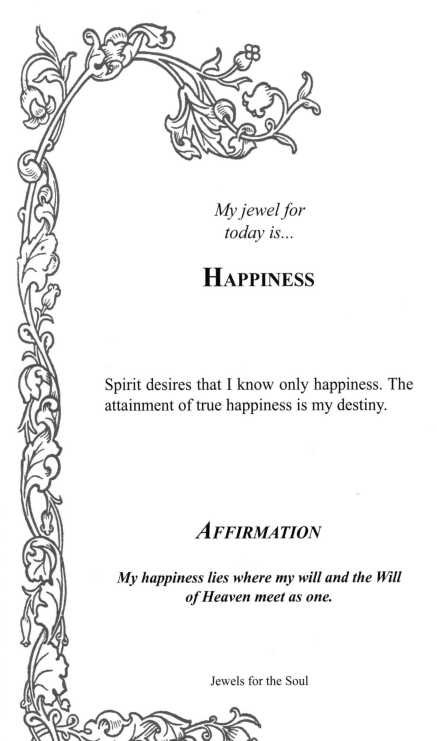

*My jewel for
today is...*

HAPPINESS

Spirit desires that I know only happiness. The attainment of true happiness is my destiny.

AFFIRMATION

**My happiness lies where my will and the Will
of Heaven meet as one.**

Jewels for the Soul

*My jewel for
today is...*

HOPE

All of the peace and harmony that I long to see
made manifest on Earth is now being created
from the very fabric of these very desires.

AFFIRMATION

**Dear Spirit, from my heart, let there shine a
ray of Eternal Hope.**

Jewels for the Soul

*My jewel for
today is...*

MODERATION

As a Spiritual Warrior, I must achieve self-discipline. As I climb to higher spiritual heights, I experience a narrowing of my path. Traveling too far to the left or right may cause me to lose my Divine footing.

AFFIRMATION

**Moderation is the middle path leading to the
Spiritual Warrior's victory.**

Jewels for the Soul

My jewel for
today is...

WORSHIP

By honoring the Sacred Spirit within all living things, I worship my Creator. By cultivating the beauty of my inner and outer nature, I worship my Source.

AFFIRMATION

To worship the Great Spirit is to remain
conscious of Its Omnipresence.

Jewels for the Soul

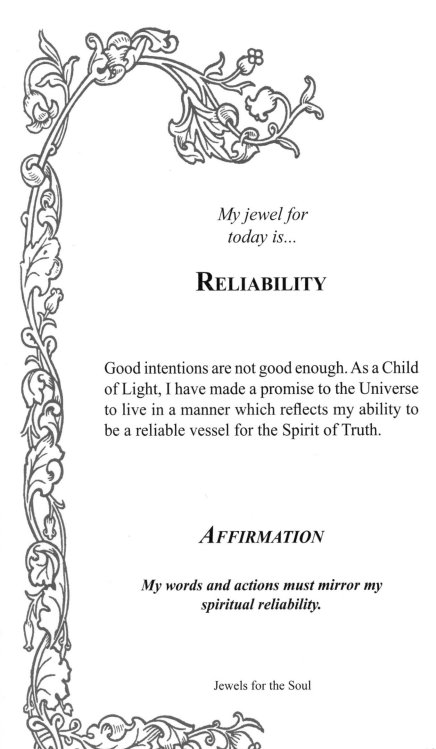

*My jewel for
today is...*

RELIABILITY

Good intentions are not good enough. As a Child
of Light, I have made a promise to the Universe
to live in a manner which reflects my ability to
be a reliable vessel for the Spirit of Truth.

AFFIRMATION

**My words and actions must mirror my
spiritual reliability.**

Jewels for the Soul

*My jewel for
today is...*

INDEPENDENCE

Although there is only one Spirit animating all
life forms upon this planet, my mind, body, and
earth mission are highly unique. I am one of
a kind. Therefore, I cannot allow myself to be
bound by the personal truth of anyone else.

AFFIRMATION

**Living my personal vision requires
spiritual independence.**

Jewels for the Soul

My jewel for
today is...

REINVENTION

My personality is the product of my combined life experiences, heretofore. I can choose at any time, to reinvent myself. If I want to be more robust or more calm, that change is just a decision away.

AFFIRMATION

The privilege of reinventing myself is granted me
by the living power of Spirit.

Jewels for the Soul

*My jewel for
today is...*

PLAYFULNESS

It is only in the openness of childlike wonder that I will experience the pure joy of Heaven on Earth. To giggle, to be playful and innocent, is my passport to spiritual bliss.

AFFIRMATION

To exhibit playfulness is to feel Divine.

Jewels for the Soul

*My jewel for
today is...*

CONSCIOUS BREATHING

The body I inhabit is nourished by food, water, and air. Inhaling the cosmic breath of life deeply and consciously is as important as eating whole foods and drinking pure water.

AFFIRMATION

Being conscious of my breathing keeps me conscious of the vital Life Force within me.

Jewels for the Soul

*My jewel for
today is...*

INNER VISION

As I give my attention to newspapers and
television, I receive a most unsettling picture
of the outer world. Yet, through my inner
vision, I can view the world more positively.

AFFIRMATION

**Divine Spirit creates only pictures of love and
light for my inner vision.**

Jewels for the Soul

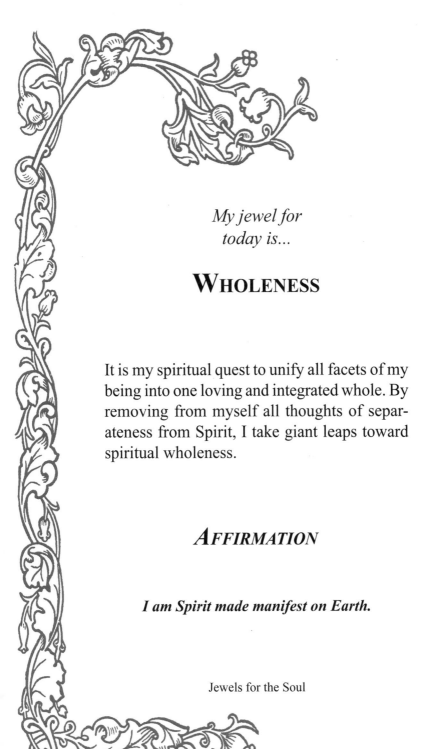

*My jewel for
today is...*

WHOLENESS

It is my spiritual quest to unify all facets of my being into one loving and integrated whole. By removing from myself all thoughts of separateness from Spirit, I take giant leaps toward spiritual wholeness.

AFFIRMATION

I am Spirit made manifest on Earth.

Jewels for the Soul

141

*My jewel for
today is...*

MEDITATION

Only in the eye of the hurricane can peace and quiet be found. Life in the outer world often resembles the chaos of a hurricane. The art of meditation removes me from the outer storm and offers me the true serenity residing within the center of my soul.

AFFIRMATION

**Through the art of meditation, I find my
home in serenity.**

Jewels for the Soul

*My jewel for
today is...*

ILLUMINATION

In truth, I am a Light Being. Today, I will sit quietly, envisioning my Light body. It is brilliant and perfect. Once I visualize it, I will increase the brightness of my Light body until it illuminates my physical body as well.

AFFIRMATION

**I am illuminated from the inside out by the
radiance of Divine Spirit.**

Jewels for the Soul

My jewel for
today is...

Oneness With Nature

Sitting beside a large old tree, near a rolling stream, or upon an ancient boulder is an excellent way to exchange energy and forge a lasting bond with the natural powers on Earth.

Affirmation

I am spiritually grounded by time spent in the splendor of nature.

Jewels for the Soul

*My jewel for
today is...*

PERFECT ALIGNMENT

The Universe is a place of Divine Order. I have traveled to Earth in order to perfect my ability to align my physical being with the spiritual perfection of the cosmos.

AFFIRMATION

**Universal perfection is now and has always
been my reality.**

Jewels for the Soul

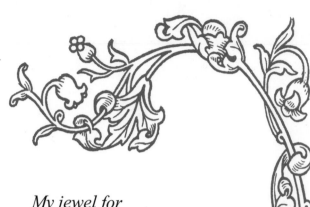

*My jewel for
today is...*

PERSONAL EXPANSION

There are innumerable paths up the mountainside of enlightenment. My spiritual philosophy may be enhanced and expanded by studying the wisdoms sacred to other peoples and cultures.

AFFIRMATION

I inspire my personal expansion by investigating other spiritual beliefs held dear by my global family.

Jewels for the Soul

*My jewel for
today is...*

VISION

As a Spiritual Warrior, I seek to view life as through the eyes of Spirit. As I succeed at witnessing the innocence and divinity inherent in all things, an exhilarating panorama of love and purpose unfold before me.

AFFIRMATION

When my spiritual eyes are focused, I behold only visions of endless love.

Jewels for the Soul

*My jewel for
today is...*

WISDOM

Through my studies and meditations, the words of the Masters flood my being with the light of consciousness. Yet, only when I courageously live in the light of truth do I attain genuine wisdom.

AFFIRMATION

*I am wise when the words of the Masters become
my living testament.*

Jewels for the Soul

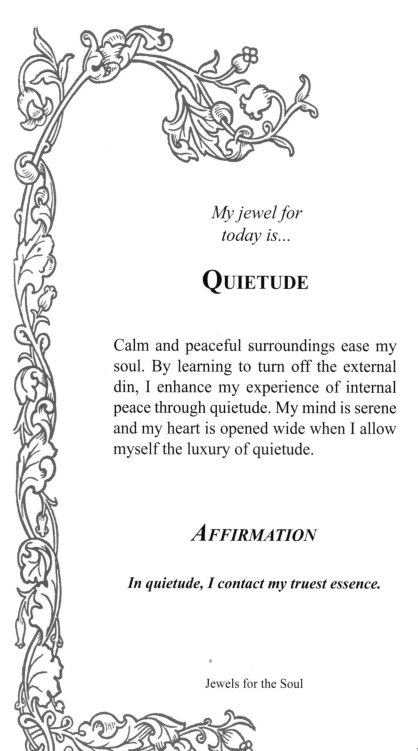

*My jewel for
today is...*

QUIETUDE

Calm and peaceful surroundings ease my
soul. By learning to turn off the external
din, I enhance my experience of internal
peace through quietude. My mind is serene
and my heart is opened wide when I allow
myself the luxury of quietude.

AFFIRMATION

In quietude, I contact my truest essence.

Jewels for the Soul

*My jewel for
today is...*

LESSON LEARNING

I am consciously cooperating with my spiritual
evolution when I believe that every circumstance
in my life has been attracted to introduce me to
yet another aspect of Infinite Intelligence.

AFFIRMATION

***Dear Spirit, bless my awareness with the Divine
Intelligence creating my every experience.***

Jewels for the Soul

*My jewel for
today is...*

QUESTING

I liken my life to the quest of the knights of old.
I too, search for the Holy Grail, that sacred cup,
said to hold the secret of eternal life. My search,
however, does not take me far and away. Instead,
it leads me to the inner sanctum.

AFFIRMATION

**My quest for eternal life begins and ends with
the discovery of my indwelling Spirit.**

Jewels for the Soul

*My jewel for
today is...*

REJOICING

Every day that I spend on Earth is a festive occasion
worthy of celebration. As I mature spiritually, my
capacity for experiencing joy deepens.

AFFIRMATION

***As I rejoice in the living of my life, I
glorify Spirit.***

Jewels for the Soul

*My jewel for
today is...*

LETTING GO

It is human nature for me to hang onto the habits and hopes of yesterday. Yet, my Divine Nature asks that I live totally in the now while I prepare myself to receive the gifts and blessings awaiting me.

AFFIRMATION

I continually manifest my highest good as I let go and let Divine Spirit flow through me.

Jewels for the Soul

*My jewel for
today is...*

THOUGHTFUL THINKING

How often I find myself contemplating thoughts representing less than the highest good for myself and others. As I remind myself that thoughts are things, I need to be more thoughtful of the things I am creating.

AFFIRMATION

**Infinite Spirit, please help me to consistently live
in Your loving thoughts.**

Jewels for the Soul

*My jewel for
today is...*

THE CHILD WITHIN

Infinite Mind manifests in me as limitless imagination. The child within is most gifted at the use of this imagination, weaving magical dreams of Heaven on Earth.

AFFIRMATION

**Through the child within, I recapture the magic
of my being.**

Jewels for the Soul

*My jewel for
today is...*

FEELING GOOD

My mind has the power to influence the health of my body and harmony of my emotions. As I mentally resolve to live fully and enjoy all aspects of my day, I align myself more easily with positive Universal energy.

AFFIRMATION

**Feeling good in body and spirit is simply a matter
of adopting a positive state of mind.**

Jewels for the Soul

*My jewel for
today is...*

POLITENESS

As an individuation of Infinite Spirit, I am a child of majesty. In remembering my royal inheritance, I must never forget my spiritual decorum. With a demeanor of courtliness, I must address each member of my Earth family with politeness, no matter what the circumstance.

AFFIRMATION

As an emissary of Spirit, I display genuine politeness through all my personal interchanges.

Jewels for the Soul

*My jewel for
today is...*

UNLEARNING

Of all the tasks before me on my path toward spiritual mastery, unlearning is the most challenging task of all. To unlearn the lessons of my youth, to unlearn the beliefs of my original family, is indeed formidable.

AFFIRMATION

With conscious effort I will position myself to unlearn any and all beliefs that do not support my present level of spiritual awareness.

Jewels for the Soul

My jewel for
today is...

FEARLESSNESS

I am a Spiritual Warrior, pledged to the preservation of Universal Life. My Earth assignment demands that I be fearless in my personal propagation of peace and unconditional love.

AFFIRMATION

There is no greater power than love, and I will be
fearless as I live my life in service
to Love's power.

Jewels for the Soul

*My jewel for
today is...*

WONDER

Everywhere I travel upon this sacred sphere called
Earth, I find myself enraptured with the wonder of
the scenic and natural beauty surrounding me. Planet
Earth is one of a kind, deserving to be appreciated
for the unselfish sharing of her grandeur.

AFFIRMATION

**Sweet Spirit, allow my heart to embrace, with
gratitude, the wonder of life on Earth.**

Jewels for the Soul

*My jewel for
today is...*

Magnetic Mental Power

It is the Spiritual Warrior's responsibility to monitor all thoughts passing through the conscious mind. One soul's prolonged consideration of human lack and limitation can cause detriment to the world at large. Thoughts possess a highly magnetic power. They attract to the soul the very substance of their contemplation.

Affirmation

I long to know Heaven on Earth, therefore, I will focus my mind on love alone.

Jewels for the Soul

*My jewel for
today is...*

HUMAN CONNECTEDNESS

As a member of humanity, I am separate from no one, and from nothing that touches the lives of my human family. Every emotion and circumstance experienced by a member of my humanity is experienced by me. I am one with Spirit, and Spirit is one with every living soul.

AFFIRMATION

***I am connected to all that lives, I am One
with all life***

Jewels for the Soul

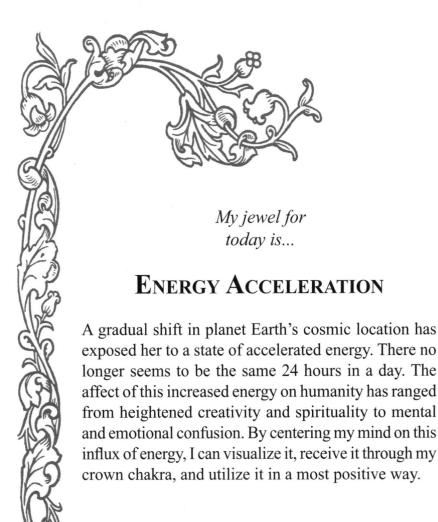

*My jewel for
today is...*

ENERGY ACCELERATION

A gradual shift in planet Earth's cosmic location has exposed her to a state of accelerated energy. There no longer seems to be the same 24 hours in a day. The affect of this increased energy on humanity has ranged from heightened creativity and spirituality to mental and emotional confusion. By centering my mind on this influx of energy, I can visualize it, receive it through my crown chakra, and utilize it in a most positive way.

AFFIRMATION

As above, so below.

Jewels for the Soul

163

*My jewel for
today is...*

EXPECTANCY

As I learn to fully trust the loving energy of Spirit, I cease to struggle with the ups and downs of physical life. As challenges arise in life, I simply turn within, always expecting Spirit to provide me, unfailingly, with enlightened guidance.

AFFIRMATION

By living in a state of perpetual expectancy, I prepare myself to receive spiritual illumination.

Jewels for the Soul

*My jewel for
today is...*

EARTH STEWARDSHIP

For many thousands of years, the Earth Mother has given of Herself unselfishly in order to assist the evolution of humankind. Now, as Her child, I must do all I can to assist Her. Caring for my personal environment, planting and nurturing all types of living things, as well as learning to recycle is an excellent beginning.

AFFIRMATION

I am an Earth Steward, and the Mother's chances for survival increase as my consciousness increases.

Jewels for the Soul

*My jewel for
today is...*

CALMNESS

On a daily basis, I am confronted with situations that test my patience and challenge my spiritual skills. Becoming flustered or angry causes me to scatter my personal energies in a manner that is counter-productive to the highest good of all concerned.

AFFIRMATION

A state of inner calmness is my strongest ally in all situations that confront me.

Jewels for the Soul

*My jewel for
today is...*

MY UNIQUENESS

Though my DNA is encoded with the same racial and universal data as everyone else's, the way I spontaneously express myself is utterly unique. There is no one else quite like me. There shall never be. I need to appreciate myself for my matchless qualities and my unparalleled representation of Holy Spirit on Earth.

AFFIRMATION

**I am at my spiritual best when I honor
my uniqueness.**

Jewels for the Soul

*My jewel for
today is...*

SELF-HEALING

An imbalance within my mind or soul will manifest as the discomfort of a disease within my body. Yet, I have the Spirit given ability to heal myself through the power of positive thought energy. As I project only loving thoughts toward myself and others, I leave no place for imbalance to survive.

AFFIRMATION

**Self-healing naturally follows as I step more
fully into my oneness in love with
Indwelling Spirit.**

Jewels for the Soul

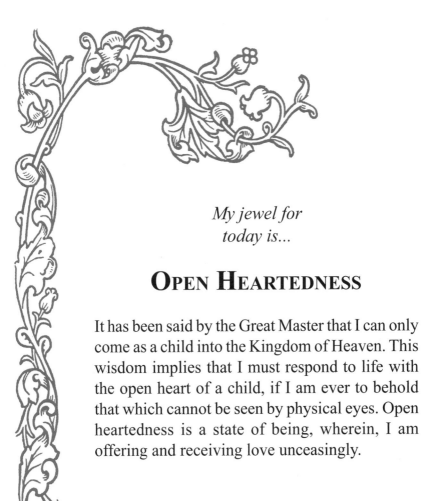

*My jewel for
today is...*

OPEN HEARTEDNESS

It has been said by the Great Master that I can only come as a child into the Kingdom of Heaven. This wisdom implies that I must respond to life with the open heart of a child, if I am ever to behold that which cannot be seen by physical eyes. Open heartedness is a state of being, wherein, I am offering and receiving love unceasingly.

AFFIRMATION

**I now open my heart to give and receive the
abundant blessings of infinite Love.**

Jewels for the Soul

*My jewel for
today is...*

GOING BEYOND KARMA

I realize that within this universe that law of cause and effect abides. Every student of truth learns this in their earliest studies. As I approach a more advanced level of spiritual understanding, I begin to perceive my ability to transcend karma. By the power of positive thought energy I can minimize the influence that karma exerts over my life's journey.

AFFIRMATION

*I am made in the image of love, and the power of love
transcends cause and effect.*

Jewels for the Soul

*My jewel for
today is...*

SUPPORTIVE FRIENDSHIP

I have many friends, for many different reasons. Some are friends because we share similar ideas and philosophies. Others are friends of mine because we work or play together. The friends dearest to me are those who know my soul, as I know theirs. We support one another's spiritual growth. These friends enrich my life, enhance my well-being, and bless me with happiness.

AFFIRMATION

***Supportive friendships represent hallowed ground
upon my spiritual path.***

Jewels for the Soul

171

*My jewel for
today is...*

SIMPLE PLEASURES

In this period of high tech, state of the art living, it is easy to misplace my capacity for slowing down to enjoy life's simple pleasures. Frolicking in a pile of fallen leaves or baking cookies with friends and family are both examples of simple pleasures, that allow me to reconnect with what is most basic, most beautiful about life.

AFFIRMATION

**The greatest truth in life is the simplest to
comprehend.**

Jewels for the Soul

*My jewel for
today is...*

ENDING PROCRASTINATION

As a Light Worker upon Planet Earth today, I find myself in a very unique position. The luxury of unlimited time is no longer mine. I cannot afford to put off until tomorrow what I need to do today. Every day I live, and through every action I take, I must be ever mindful of the Will of Heaven.

AFFIRMATION

**I will end procrastination for it serves to weaken
my spiritual resolve.**

Jewels for the Soul

173

*My jewel for
today is...*

CONQUERING FEAR

In the presence of Light, no darkness can exist. As a Spiritual Warrior, I can follow only one master. If love is my master and guiding light, fear has no power in my life except that which I give it.

AFFIRMATION

*I conquer my fears by focusing my mind on
the Light of Spirit.*

Jewels for the Soul

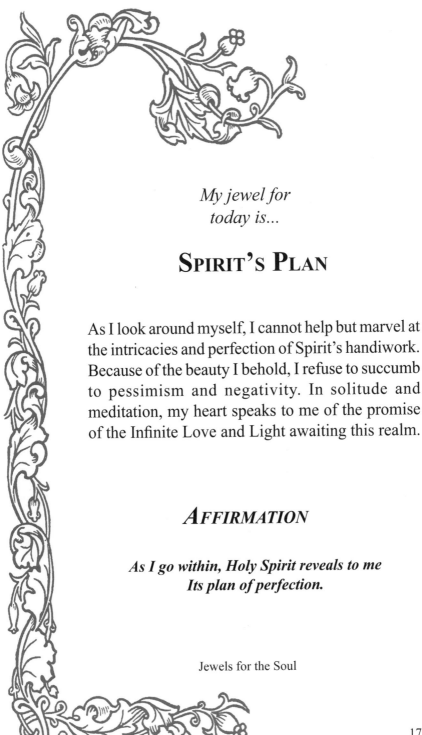

*My jewel for
today is...*

SPIRIT'S PLAN

As I look around myself, I cannot help but marvel at
the intricacies and perfection of Spirit's handiwork.
Because of the beauty I behold, I refuse to succumb
to pessimism and negativity. In solitude and
meditation, my heart speaks to me of the promise
of the Infinite Love and Light awaiting this realm.

AFFIRMATION

**As I go within, Holy Spirit reveals to me
Its plan of perfection.**

Jewels for the Soul

*My jewel for
today is...*

HONORING UNIVERSAL CYCLES

I am one with the All That Is. Therefore, it is my destiny to honor the universal cycles of change. If I should resist the occurrence of life-cycles, I deplete my precious energy, and I am left feeling at odds with life. As I honor theses cycles, I am filled with flowing energy and a thirst for life well-lived.

AFFIRMATION

*I allow my life to be perfected by the blessing
flowing forth with each cosmic
cycle of change.*

Jewels for the Soul

*My jewel for
today is...*

LISTENING TO MY BODY

There are many demands placed upon Light Workers. I have my own growth and evolution to nurture as well as my responsibilities to the greater family. When so much is happening, on a daily basis, it is quite easy for me to overlook my need for rest. I must learn to listen and respond consistently to my body, with physical, emotional, and spiritual nourishment.

AFFIRMATION

**Listening to my body is paramount to my
success as a Light Worker.**

Jewels for the Soul

*My jewel for
today is...*

MY POTENTIAL

I have been sent to Earth by the Universal Powers in order to expand my awareness and magnify my potential for love. As a spark from the Mother-Father-God, I am capable of doing all things. However, my Earth assignment directs me to focus most fully on those things, that by doing well, I bring to myself and the world greater joy.

AFFIRMATION

*I live up to my Infinite Potential by experiencing
and spreading spiritual joy.*

Jewels for the Soul

*My jewel for
today is...*

EXCITEMENT

I am living in one of the most exciting times of growth ever known on Earth. All around me, freedom and equity are demanding their place in the world. Higher thought is finding its way into the world's music, art, and literature. More and more of my brothers and sisters are becoming inspired to commence their individual quests for peace of mind through spiritual understanding.

AFFIRMATION

**Holy One, I ask that you continually renew my
spirit with Divine excitement.**

Jewels for the Soul

My jewel for
today is...

AFFIRMATIONS

Replacing old, self-limiting tapes, in my unconscious, with new, enlightened messages, is a vital exercise for the Spiritual Warrior. By affirming my greatest good as the outcome to every challenge I face, I elevate my conscious awareness of Spirit. By doing this, I also elevate the frequency of the challenge so that it is no longer in conflict with my personal energy.

AFFIRMATION

Affirmations are a magical key for transforming
my world.

Jewels for the Soul

*My jewel for
today is...*

THE COSMIC MOTHER

I could never know myself in totality, without coming to know the Mother of One Thousand Names. The Supreme Feminine Power of the Cosmos has been known to every culture since time immemorial. She is the Blessed One on High, birthing universes and bringing them to maturity through Her Infinite love and compassion. Her Spirit shines brightly within every man, woman, and child.

AFFIRMATION

*Great Mother, hold me close and guide me to the full
knowledge of myself through our
intimate association.*

Jewels for the Soul

*My jewel for
today is...*

I Am

There is but one I Am and I am a part of Its eternal greatness. Like a single droplet dancing in the endless sea, I am one with The Infinite.

AFFIRMATION

*I Am, and what I Am is pure love and light due
to the power and presence of
Spirit within me.*

Jewels for the Soul

*My jewel for
today is...*

BEING PERFECT

As a Light worker, I have been sent from another world or dimension to assist the earth in her upliftment. It is part of my spiritual responsibility to manifest the perfection of the Holy Spirit on Earth.

AFFIRMATION

Mother-Father God, as an ambassador in your sacred legion, I will proudly seek to present Your perfection in all I say and do.

Jewels for the Soul

*My jewel for
today is...*

BEGINNER'S EYE

The beginner's eye is unclouded. As I behold the world around me, ever changing, ever new, I need to remember to see it through the beginner's eye. I cannot measure today by yesterday's standard. As each new day dawns, I am recreated. As I reach my zenith with the noon Sun, and unwind with its setting, I still must cleave to the beginner's eye within me, untainted and unprejudiced.

AFFIRMATION

**The beginner's eye is my passport into the
Kingdom of Heaven.**

Jewels for the Soul

*My jewel for
today is...*

DETACHED EMPATHY

Empathy is a divine quality longing to find its way into every human heart. However, by becoming attached to having empathy, oft times, I paralyze my ability to contribute healing to the person or situation in need. Empathy reflects my personal understanding of emotion. Detached empathy reaches beyond emotion, to the solutions found in the Heart of Spirit.

AFFIRMATION

***Detaching from emotion frees my soul to work
spiritual miracles.***

Jewels for the Soul

*My jewel for
today is...*

UNIVERSAL CONNECTEDNESS

As I aspire to ever greater levels of spiritual awareness, I gently come into a consciousness of Universal Connectedness. I am one with the sky and the moon. I am part of the ocean and the earth. All life is energy, all energy is consciousness.

AFFIRMATION

*My consciousness expands to include
The Infinite as I tap into my
Universal Connection.*

Jewels for the Soul

*My jewel for
today is...*

Experiencing The Pain

It is human nature to think of interfering with life when it appears that pain and suffering are on the horizon. Yet, it is the wisdom of Spirit to allow the experience of pain to have its full expression, when and where it has been summoned.

Affirmation

I willfully experience the pain I have attracted as I simultaneously affirm that all future growth will be precipitated only by joy.

Jewels for the Soul

*My jewel for
today is...*

LIVING IN THE PRESENCE

While I busy myself each day with the business of life in the physical realm, it is in my highest interest to maintain a conscious awareness of my oneness with the Great I Am. All crooked places are made straight, and life is enchanted, when I live in the awareness that it is in this Divine presence that I live, move, and have my being.

AFFIRMATION

**Life is never more beautiful than when I
remember that I am living in the
I Am presence.**

Jewels for the Soul

*My jewel for
today is...*

INFLUENCE

It is an integral part of my Earth assignment
to make my loving and inspired influence felt.
It is not enough for me to attain wisdom and
emotional mastery this time around. I must also
endeavor to influence the lives of others in the
most positive and constructive way possible.

AFFIRMATION

**My spiritual savvy must be used as an uplifting
influence for the good of all.**

Jewels for the Soul

*My jewel for
today is...*

White Light Infusion

Before I leave my bed each morning, I will close
my eyes and contact the God-Mind deep within me.
I will envision the White Light of the Upper Ray.
Through my third eye, I will direct this light into
every single cell of my being. In so doing, I infuse
my physical life with the Infinite Life of Spirit.

Affirmation

***Now and forevermore I am cradled in the sheltering
arms of Eternal Love.***

Jewels for the Soul

*My jewel for
today is...*

LIFTING THE LOAD OF THE WEARY

From time to time, we all become overwhelmed with the stresses and workload of modern living. If I can, in any way, at any time, help lift the load from one of my weary brothers or sisters, then this I must do. Offering to watch the children of a tired parent, or running errands for a sick friend are little things that can make a big difference in someone else's life.

AFFIRMATION

**As a Spiritual Warrior, I am inwardly strengthened
as I ease the burden of the weary.**

Jewels for the Soul

*My jewel for
today is...*

BELIEVING IN MYSELF

Once I comprehend, at the deepest levels of my being, that I am the perfect manifestation of godliness, I will automatically cease to doubt my worth. Accepting my identity as the physical counterpart of the Omnipotent One, I must believe in my power and greatness.

AFFIRMATION

**Believing in myself demonstrates my unwavering
faith in the Mother-Father God.**

Jewels for the Soul

*My jewel for
today is...*

COOPERATION

Working in harmony with my brothers and
sisters on Earth is not always a joyful event,
but I need to remember that it is a Holy One.
We have all been hand picked to play on
Spirit's team. Personal discord does not serve
the Will of Heaven.

AFFIRMATION

***I bring joy to Heaven and Earth as I learn to
cooperate with Life.***

Jewels for the Soul

*My jewel for
today is...*

RADIANT HEALTH

As a child of the Divine, I am to reflect the perfection of my Creator. My physical condition is one of the most obvious reflections of my spiritual state of being.

AFFIRMATION

I radiate perfect health.

Jewels for the Soul

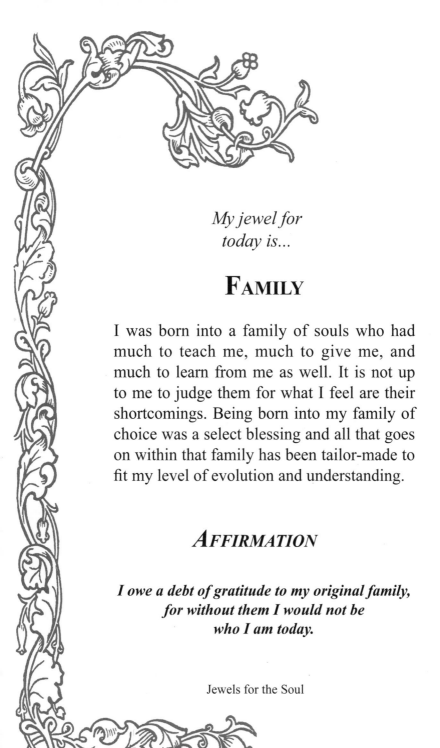

*My jewel for
today is...*

FAMILY

I was born into a family of souls who had much to teach me, much to give me, and much to learn from me as well. It is not up to me to judge them for what I feel are their shortcomings. Being born into my family of choice was a select blessing and all that goes on within that family has been tailor-made to fit my level of evolution and understanding.

AFFIRMATION

**I owe a debt of gratitude to my original family,
for without them I would not be
who I am today.**

Jewels for the Soul

*My jewel for
today is...*

WILLINGNESS

The physical realm is the launching pad into higher dimensions of thought and beingness. As a soul, venturing the path of perfection, I need to remind myself to demonstrate the willingness to be guided at every turn. I must also be willing to learn, even when every fiber within me resists.

AFFIRMATION

***I must be willing to love, even when the thought
of it seems impossible.***

Jewels for the Soul

*My jewel for
today is...*

THINKING SPIRITUALLY

What I do unto the least of my brethren, I do unto the Universal Heart. Every time I take an action, I need to think about the possible spiritual ramifications. Will my words and deeds contribute love and light, or fear and limitation to this realm? Getting into the habit of thinking with my spiritual mind will increase my vibration as well as the vibration of Planet Earth.

AFFIRMATION

*As I open my consciousness to receive thoughts from
Universal Mind, I fill the Universal
Heart with gladness.*

Jewels for the Soul

My jewel for
today is...

THE JOY OF INTIMACY

Intimacy is a gift of love unconditionally reciprocated by two people. The sharing of intimate meals and conversations, along with physical exchanges of affection are among some of the most beautiful elements of the human experience.

AFFIRMATION

I cherish the joy of intimacy as a treasured gift
from the Goddess.

Jewels for the Soul

*My jewel for
today is...*

PREPARING MYSELF AS A VESSEL

Throughout lifetime after lifetime, my soul urge has been toward the attainment of spiritual truth and enlightenment. Finding the answers to the mysteries of life has been my driving force. Preparing to serve as a vessel of goodness and integrity has been my Holy mission.

AFFIRMATION

***It is my destiny to serve as a vessel for the
light of Love.***

Jewels for the Soul

*My jewel for
today is...*

LIGHT HEARTEDNESS

When my heart feels as if it will break, and my world seems like a house full of strangers, it is then that I need to fill my heart with the Light of Spirit. Light heartedness means embracing the Light of the Christos. Where there is light, no darkness of Spirit can remain.

AFFIRMATION

I am the Light of the World.

Jewels for the Soul

*My jewel for
today is...*

THE GIFT OF LOVE

Love is the universal reality. In truth, it is the only real thing that exists. I am love and by giving of myself, I give love to the world.

AFFIRMATION

Love is the only lasting gift that I can give.

Jewels for the Soul

*My jewel for
today is...*

AUTHENTIC HUMANITY

To become an authentic human, I must fully acknowledge my physical restrictions, while fully accentuating my spiritual perfection. In order to experience authentic humanity, I must not fear the tribulations of life and, I must not shun the ecstasies inherent in life on Earth. I must face life on its own terms so that I can assist others in doing the same.

AFFIRMATION

***The authenticity of my humanness is measured by my
courage to live and let live.***

Jewels for the Soul

202

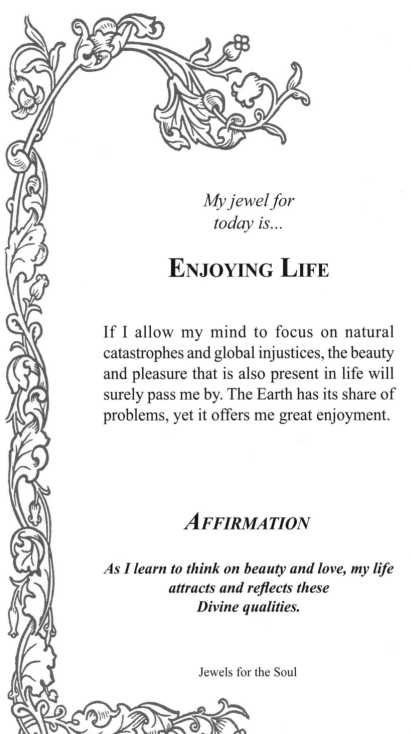

*My jewel for
today is...*

ENJOYING LIFE

If I allow my mind to focus on natural
catastrophes and global injustices, the beauty
and pleasure that is also present in life will
surely pass me by. The Earth has its share of
problems, yet it offers me great enjoyment.

AFFIRMATION

***As I learn to think on beauty and love, my life
attracts and reflects these
Divine qualities.***

Jewels for the Soul

*My jewel for
today is...*

HOLY EXPRESSION

I am a perfect thought of the Almighty. I carry within me the Light of Christ, the Love of Goddess, and the Infinite Intelligence of God. My life is immortal, my Spirit invincible. It is my destiny to express my Divinity through a life lived in dedication to the righteous principles of the Holy Spirit.

AFFIRMATION

I am the Holy expression of Spirit's perfection.

Jewels for the Soul

*My jewel for
today is...*

PUTTING THE PAST TO REST

All of my yesterdays have been packed with learning experiences and everlasting joys. As the future reaches out to embrace me, I will embrace the many happinesses I have earned, and will put away all sorrow, regret, and unclaimed baggage.

AFFIRMATION

*Leaving behind disappointment and heartbreak,
I step into all of my tomorrows with optimism,
steadfastness, and an open heart.*

Jewels for the Soul

*My jewel for
today is...*

APPRECIATION

My blessings in life increase and multiply as I begin to acknowledge them and give thanks accordingly. By living in a state of conscious appreciation, I create more and more to be thankful for.

AFFIRMATION

**Appreciation opens the door to my
Divine Abundance.**

Jewels for the Soul

206

*My jewel for
today is...*

RADIATING MY DIVINE NATURE

The Universal Law of Attraction compels me to align my physical self with my Divine Reality. Like attracts like. As long as I radiate my Divine Nature in all my daily interchanges, it is law that I bring out the Divine in all the people and situations I encounter.

AFFIRMATION

*In radiating my Divine Nature, I light the way
for others to follow.*

Jewels for the Soul

*My jewel for
today is...*

NOT QUESTIONING WHY

The Divine Mind is so expansive, so limitless, that comprehension of it by the mortal mind is an impossible task. Therefore, the reason and purpose for every happening in the Universe is often beyond the scope of human understanding.

AFFIRMATION

**Learning to trust Infinite Intelligence is a sign of
supreme spiritual wisdom.**

Jewels for the Soul

*My jewel for
today is...*

SEEING ONLY LOVE

Everything I perceive as reality was first a product of my own mind. I project my mental pictures and attitudes onto life's blank canvas, then I experience the results of these positive or negative thought energies.

AFFIRMATION

If I choose to see only love, then love will become my only reality.

Jewels for the Soul

*My jewel for
today is...*

MY MAGNIFICENCE

I am flawless. I am the beautiful reflection of my Divine parentage. No matter what imperfection my humanness portrays, my identity as spiritual perfection is unthreatened. I am the essence of the Great I Am.

AFFIRMATION

**I am the magnificent expression of
Universal Perfection.**

Jewels for the Soul

*My jewel for
today is...*

TAKING THE FIRST STEP

Often times in life, the only thing that stands between me and my greatest victory, is the fear of taking that first step. Whether it is that diet I wish to begin, the new job I seek, or the pursuing of my dream of dreams, today I pledge to take the first step necessary. I will never know what I can accomplish if I am frozen in place by fear.

AFFIRMATION

***Today I will take the first step toward my
innate greatness.***

Jewels for the Soul

My jewel for
today is...

Daring To Be Myself

Within me there is a unique blueprint for a life purposefully lived. My mission on Earth is the rediscovery of unconditional love and the meaning of Infinite Life. As such, I must dare to be true to myself. I must follow my inner guidance no matter where it leads.

Affirmation

I manifest the power of Infinite Spirit when I
dare to be myself.

Jewels for the Soul

*My jewel for
today is...*

CREATING A LIFE OF LOVE

I am the creative force at the center of my personal universe. Everything that transpires in my world is a direct response to my dominant thoughts and actions. My desire to create a life of love dictates that I recreate my world of thoughts and emotions.

AFFIRMATION

From this day forward, I will give energy to only those thoughts and emotions which empower love and harmony in my life.

Jewels for the Soul

*My jewel for
today is...*

EXERCISING MY THIRD EYE

As I unfold to my spiritual nature, learning to
see without my physical eyes is imperative.
First I need to see myself through my spiritual
eyes, then I can behold the spiritual essence of
the world around me. So, for my first exercise:
periodically, throughout the day, I shall close
my eyes and behold my inbeing clothed in the
Seven Rays of Divine Realization.

AFFIRMATION

**I love and appreciate myself more fully as I
view my reality through the clarity
of my third eye.**

Jewels for the Soul

*My jewel for
today is...*

SPIRITUAL RENEWAL

This is a perfect day to renew my spirit. If I allow myself to spend time in contemplation of spiritual matters, I will surely find myself renewed. Reflecting on my true nature as a child of Infinite Love acts to strengthen and inspire me. Time spent in deep meditation today, will enable me to focus my thoughts and energies in the days ahead.

AFFIRMATION

**I am spiritually renewed by time quietly spent in
the I Am Presence.**

Jewels for the Soul

*My jewel for
today is...*

Living In An Awakened State

Mastering the arts of prayer, meditation and surrender are all necessary steps toward my awakening. Through the use of these three Divine skills, I am enabled, every moment of every day, to remain in an awakened state of spiritual consciousness. I cannot turn back, and I cannot allow myself to lapse into the sleep of ignorance, ever again.

AFFIRMATION

Becoming aware was facile; maintaining a fully awakened state is my true test.

Jewels for the Soul

*My jewel for
today is...*

DELIBERATION

When I speak or act in haste, I am more likely
to experience remorse. However, when I
deliberately pause long enough to draw upon
the wisdom of the Goddess, I bring only honor
and truth to myself and others.

AFFIRMATION

**As I speak with the deliberation of love and
wisdom, I manifest the Goddess on Earth.**

Jewels for the Soul

*My jewel for
today is...*

CHOOSING TO BE JOYFUL

I have the ability to choose to be joyful regardless of what is going on around me. Leftover problems from yesterday and concerns about tomorrow shall not disturb my inner joy, if that is my conviction.

AFFIRMATION

*I am in control of my life and today I
choose to be joyful.*

Jewels for the Soul

*My jewel for
today is...*

MY MINISTRY

Today, the Universe has placed me in a perfect position to perform the Will of Heaven. My life is my ministry. The focus of my ministry is to bring the Golden Light of Love into focus anywhere and everywhere I find myself.

AFFIRMATION

I pledge to minister to my brothers and sisters with love and kindness all the days of my life.

Jewels for the Soul

*My jewel for
today is...*

Unlimiting Infinite Mind

Spirit desires that all my dreams come true.
Happiness, health, and abundance are indeed my
Divine Inheritance. Yet, my human mind constantly
limits the full measure of my spiritual bounty.
Through doubt and disbelief, I limit the outpouring
of Infinite Mind's blessings into my life.

AFFIRMATION

**In Infinite Mind, every blessing imaginable is
already mine.**

Jewels for the Soul

*My jewel for
today is...*

BEING FULLY ALIVE

I will experience the fullness of my life to the extent that I allow myself the honest pleasure and passion of my being. By taking risks, seeking out new adventures, and lovingly searching for the face of God in everyone I meet, I will come to intimately know the exhilaration of being fully alive.

AFFIRMATION

I am fully alive when my passion is my purpose.

Jewels for the Soul

*My jewel for
today is...*

Articulating All Goodness

My natural curiosity shows an interest in the sensational details of the nation's latest front page scandal. I know this kind of inquisitiveness is essentially meaningless. Idle talk of such tragedy multiplies the suffering of those involved.

Affirmation

Sweet Spirit, give me eyes to see and a voice to articulate all the goodness that is taking place in our world today and everyday.

Jewels for the Soul

*My jewel for
today is...*

TAKING A STAND AGAINST IGNORANCE

With open eyes, it is not difficult to see that hatred, racism, and prejudice are reaching yet another peak in popularity. The media has fanned the flames of ignorance in hopes of exposing it; however, instead it appears to have given it license, in the small minds of many. As a teacher of the truth, it is my obligation to Loving Spirit to stand up against such ignorance, anywhere and in anyway I can.

AFFIRMATION

The display of tolerance in the presence of hatred and racism acts to condone these most hideous of all human evils.

Jewels for the Soul

My jewel for
today is...

DISSOLVING MY OBSTACLES TO PEACE

Infinite Spirit has guided my immortal soul to this land of discovery for many reasons. The presence of so-called obstacles, in my life, were designed to gently lead my heart on its quest for unconditional peace. As I allow myself to become more centered in peacefulness, I find obstacles dissolve before my very eyes.

AFFIRMATION

Sweet Spirit, in my love for you I find peace
without end.

Jewels for the Soul

*My jewel for
today is...*

Being Loyal To My Word

There have been times when I said something just because I thought it was what someone needed to hear. I didn't say it because is was heartfelt or because I planned to back it up with any real action. I simply wanted to stroke an ego or smooth a few ruffled feathers. While this kind of behavior may be expeditious, it is not genuine. It manifests no honor in my spoken word. By being loyal to my word I eliminate the need for a great many future apologies.

AFFIRMATION

***Every time I open my mouth, Sweet Spirit, please help
me utter only those words to
which I can be loyal.***

Jewels for the Soul

*My jewel for
today is...*

SOFTNESS

A soft voice and a gentle answer can calm almost
any situation. I takes just as much precious time, and
even more energy, to shout out a harsh reply. With
the serenity of the angels, and the sweetness of love,
this day I will attempt to respond to every person and
circumstance with softness. For with righteousness
to support it, the strength of softness is mightier than
the sharpest sword.

AFFIRMATION

**I am made invincible by aligning myself with
Spirit through the mystical
Tao of softness.**

Jewels for the Soul

*My jewel for
today is...*

Remembering The Departed

There is a legacy of understanding and love left behind by each and every soul who ever walked the Earth. For no life was ever wasted. Every lesson ever mastered by a fellow soul, shines light on my life. Today, I take time out to remember those loved ones who have ventured beyond this realm, yet have left behind a plethora of wit and wisdom from which I might draw a bit of strength and serenity.

AFFIRMATION

***Today, I will contemplate the lives of those departed
and I will be grateful for the priceless gifts that
their lives have bequeathed me.***

Jewels for the Soul

*My jewel for
today is...*

EMOTIONAL SELF-PROTECTION

As I feel myself opening to the Universe, I more fully understand the concept of unconditional love and the relativity of physical reality. At the same time I must learn to accept the fact that everyone I meet will not share my exact philosophy. Opposing and diverse frequencies of thought will bombard my sacred space daily. Therefore, I shall not leave myself vulnerable and emotionally unprotected.

AFFIRMATION

***Each day before I step into the outer world, I shall
shield myself with the White Light of
loving protection.***

Jewels for the Soul

*My jewel for
today is...*

THE ETERNAL

Deceiving appearances abound in this physical realm of shadows. What is real and lasting is not always obvious to the human eye. It is my responsibility to tear away the veil of mystery in order to catch a glimpse of the Eternal. Truth remains forever. Love can never pass away. Spirit is Infinite. In these eternal constants, I will place my faith and trust.

AFFIRMATION

I am one with Eternal Love, Light, and Life.

Jewels for the Soul

*My jewel for
today is...*

EXUBERANCE

In all the cosmos, there is positively nothing more thrilling than the presence of spiritual exuberance. While basking in the sparkle of this awesome quality, one is magically transported to the heavenly kingdoms. To emanate spiritual exuberance is to emulate the passionate nature of the Universal Creative Principle. In all ways, I will seek to bring exuberance to my life tasks, my personal being, and my sacred space.

AFFIRMATION

**The power and glory of Spirit is made manifest in
my exuberance for life.**

Jewels for the Soul

*My jewel for
today is...*

RIGHTEOUSNESS

As I endeavor to live my life by the Golden Rule,
I aim my sights on a life of righteousness. In being
equitable in all my dealings, I show respect for
the Will of Heaven. By attempting to do what is
morally correct under any and all circumstances,
I pay homage to my spiritual lineage.

AFFIRMATION

Righteousness is my spiritual path.

Jewels for the Soul

*My jewel for
today is...*

RETURNING TO MY SPIRITUAL ROOTS

It matters little into which ethnic or cultural group I was born. My family of origin is the Family of God. My spiritual roots travel deep into the heart of time and space. They are not limited to a small division of land here on Earth. I am a cherished member of the Universal family, where my ties are cosmic and unbreakable.

AFFIRMATION

**My spiritual roots bind me eternally to the
Oneness of all life.**

Jewels for the Soul

*My jewel for
today is...*

SEEING THE OTHER SIDE

So many arguments and friendship estrangements occur due to the fact that I fail to recognize the other side of an issue. Being trapped by my own feelings restricts me from perceiving the myriad of options available to me. I limit my own growth by stubbornly closing my heart to new and alternative possibilities in thought. To be truly wise is to be informed. I limit my wisdom when I consider only a single point of view.

AFFIRMATION

Becoming a true visionary begins by learning to see life from all sides.

Jewels for the Soul

233

*My jewel for
today is...*

FOREGOING STRUGGLE

For this one day, I promise myself that no matter what conflict or inconvenience confronts me, I shall forego the inclination to struggle against it. I will flow with all situations in a mindful, fluid manner. I will stay attuned to the stress levels in my body, reminding myself to breathe deeply and release all tension swiftly. Sacrificing my need for struggle will free my mind and heart for more pleasurable activities.

AFFIRMATION

**To struggle is human, to forego struggle is the
way of the Divine.**

Jewels for the Soul

*My jewel for
today is...*

SELFISHNESS

In all my bold and caring attempts to contribute my share on behalf of my human family, I must not forget to nurture myself. Acts of loving selfishness, such as time alone, saying no when necessary, and asking for what I need, are imperative for a spiritual Light Worker. There will be times when I will only be able to nurture the world, by nurturing myself.

AFFIRMATION

*As I practice regular acts of selfishness, I bathe my
spirit in the splendor of self-love.*

Jewels for the Soul

235

*My jewel for
today is...*

GENEROSITY

I enjoy many blessings in my life. The Universe is ever ready to grant my heartfelt wishes and support my loftiest dreams. For this reason, it is my great good fortune to share of myself with those souls who cross my path and touch my life. It blesses the entire Universe whenever I assist and inspire another soul upon their journey toward wholeness. The spirit of generosity is part of my Divine Inheritance.

AFFIRMATION

**To be generous with my time, energy and
encouragement, on behalf of
another, is an act of love.**

Jewels for the Soul

My jewel for
today is...

MY UNLIMITED POWER

When I was a young child, the world seemed so vast yet so accessible. I imagined one day I could learn to fly or scale the highest mountain known to man. I even dreamed of discovering a cure for all disease. Yet, today I am older and I still know that nothing is beyond my scope of vision, for I believe, nothing is beyond my grasp.

AFFIRMATION

Miracles begin and end with the unlimited power
of my imagination.

Jewels for the Soul

*My jewel for
today is...*

INTUITIVE GUIDANCE

If I allow it, my intuitive essence guides me throughout the day. Yet, every petty thought I think, and each negative word I speak, stands as a barrier directly between me and my spiritual intuition. Gradually, with love, I need to reposition my intellect to release ego so that it no longer interferes with the loving issue of my intuitive guidance.

AFFIRMATION

**My intuition is merely the all-knowing
whisper of Spirit.**

Jewels for the Soul

238

*My jewel for
today is...*

BEING A BRINGER OF GLAD TIDINGS

Into each life, disappointment, loss and unhappiness find their way. I cannot allow any state of frustration to become a way of life for me. The appearance of a difficult circumstance is simply a temporary expression of a physical challenge brought on by spiritual myopia.

AFFIRMATION

**As a Spiritual Warrior, it is my quest to be a bringer
of glad tidings into a world too
often colored with sorrow.**

Jewels for the Soul

*My jewel for
today is...*

Sharing My Love

To fully comprehend my spiritual nature, I must begin to experience the full force of the power of love. Sharing my love with those who share my life, my path, and my vision is part of my destiny. I share my love by patiently giving of my heart and soul in whatever way suits the life event at hand.

Affirmation

The Love of Sprit is ceaseless and unending; the more I share my love, the more I have to share.

Jewels for the Soul

*My jewel for
today is...*

BANISHING WORRY

If I truly comprehend that within the Universe there
is only One Loving Spirit, One Unlimited Source,
dedicated to my happiness and well-being, then why
do I so often give way to worry? Worry is nothing more
than doubt. Doubt is a direct lack of faith. Furthermore,
over time, worry's personal vibration will erect a very
tall wall between me and my Highest Good.

AFFIRMATION

*This day I shall replace all worrisome thoughts with
seeds of faith planted firmly in the fertile
soil of Infinite Supply.*

Jewels for the Soul

*My jewel for
today is...*

COMMUNICATION WITH THE INFINITE

Within my being there dwells the essence and presence of Supreme Perfection. I am part of All That Is. I have the precious ability to communicate with The Infinite by stilling my mind through meditation, empowering my soul through prayer, and by opening my heart through the purifying Light of Love.

AFFIRMATION

At all times, Infinite Mind stands ready and willing to commune with my Spirit.

Jewels for the Soul

*My jewel for
today is...*

Penetrating The Veil of Wickedness

If ever I should become a target of hateful lies and viciousness, I must remain unshaken, Another's evil attack is nothing more than a display of their self-loathing. The measure of one's wickedness is always manifested in direct proportion to their internal pain.

Affirmation

**In the presence of wickedness, I shall perceive the
underlying pain, and react with compassion.**

Jewels for the Soul

*My jewel for
today is...*

ENHANCING MY EARTHLY EXPERIENCE

I know that my life has purpose and meaning. I arrived on Earth with a great and wondrous spiritual plan for the promotion of my personal evolution through the contribution of my God-given talents. I must use these talents for the benefit of all humankind. I enhance the pleasure of my Earthly experience by giving back to the world as much as I receive from Spirit.

AFFIRMATION

**My life is enhanced by all the love and joy I
manage to give away.**

Jewels for the Soul

*My jewel for
today is...*

MY RESURRECTION

All life is part of the Eternal. Death, as we perceive it, does not exist, for life energy cannot be annihilated. The symbology of resurrection is used to instruct us that no matter how long we have been asleep to the truth of our Divine identity, we have the ability to rise in consciousness whenever we choose. Our lives can become holy instruments of love once we grasp our eternal oneness with the Infinite.

AFFIRMATION

***I am resurrected by my conscious acceptance of my
Oneness with Divine Spirit.***

Jewels for the Soul

*My jewel for
today is...*

ACCENTUATING THE POSITIVE

There are so many marvelous people and things in my life that deserve celebrating. I cannot allow myself to ever get stuck in neutral because everything is not going along according to my will. It is the Will of Heaven that I long to serve. And I do that best by accentuating the positive that resides in each and every moment I live.

AFFIRMATION

My positive outlook is a loving tribute to the Great Cosmic Mother.

Jewels for the Soul

*My jewel for
today is...*

SEEKING OUT LIKE MINDS

It is such a joy to find like minds with which to share my spiritual philosophies. In the exulted presence of Higher Thought my soul takes flight. I am elevated to new heights of inspiration when I surround myself, on a regular basis, with other souls dedicated to the pursuit of truth and enlightenment.

AFFIRMATION

**Loving Spirit, lead me this day, to kindred souls
of like mind.**

Jewels for the Soul

*My jewel for
today is...*

FINDING HARMONY AMID CHAOS

So often in life, things seem to get out of control. Life becomes too hectic as outer demands on my time and energy never seem to cease. In these times, it is imperative that I turn within to seek harmony at the center of my being. Amid all outer chaos, there is peace within. Instead of struggling in the abyss of confusion, I need to train myself to go, automatically, to this sacred space, in times of disequilibrium.

AFFIRMATION

***As I flounder in chaos, I create more of the
same, therefore instead, I turn within to
bathe myself in God's peace.***

Jewels for the Soul

*My jewel for
today is...*

Maintaining My Temple

My physical body is my spiritual vehicle. The foods I feed it need to be alive in order to nourish my living temple. The thoughts I think about my body must be positive in order to support its optimum functioning. The exercise I give it must be regular and enjoyable in order for my body to benefit. The rest I offer my body must be peaceful and consistent so that internal order is preserved. Maintaining my temple is a sacred responsibility.

AFFIRMATION

**The quality of my spiritual life depends,
in great part, upon how I maintain
my temple.**

Jewels for the Soul

*My jewel for
today is...*

PROSPERITY'S SPIRITUAL NATURE

As I pay attention to those around me, often I hear them expressing that money is not a spiritual thing to possess, and that people who have abundant income are somehow less spiritual than those still struggling with finances. This is a false and dangerous concept. For me to live a prosperous and abundant life is the Will of Heaven. There is nothing spiritual about living in a consciousness of lack and limitation.

AFFIRMATION

I know that I have reached spiritual maturity when I possess abundant good health, happiness, and financial prosperity.

Jewels for the Soul

*My jewel for
today is...*

TAPPING INTO UNIVERSAL MIND

Anyone who is capable of seeing into the future or the past is doing this by tapping into the Universal Mind. It would seem that psychics and sensitives have a direct line to Spirit, yet, this line is accessible to me as well. By acknowledging that there is only One Universal Mind and that I am part of it, I can learn to connect with the Universe at will. All knowledge and information, meaningful to me, is available if only I seek to find it.

AFFIRMATION

**As my Spirit seeks Oneness with the Holy
Spirit, through prayer and meditation, my mind
automatically finds Oneness with the
Universal Mind.**

Jewels for the Soul

251

*My jewel for
today is...*

STANDING ON FAITH

At times I feel I have done all I can to reach my spiritual goals, and still, I've come up short. Life simply is not what I want it to be. It seems, that with all I have studied and all I've tried, I am not living the spiritual life I long for. Well, the good news is, that everyone goes through these phases of feeling spiritually stagnant. During these periods I must stand on faith, knowing steadfastly that my sincere efforts will manifest richly, in the right and perfect time.

AFFIRMATION

**The depth and measure of my faith will determine the
bounty of my spiritual life.**

Jewels for the Soul

252

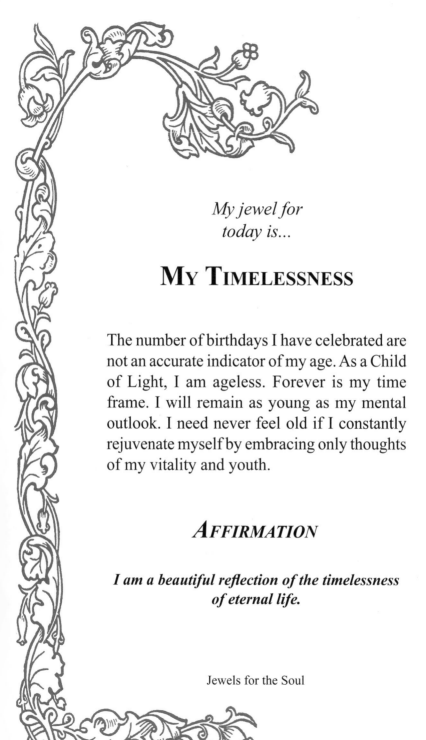

*My jewel for
today is...*

MY TIMELESSNESS

The number of birthdays I have celebrated are not an accurate indicator of my age. As a Child of Light, I am ageless. Forever is my time frame. I will remain as young as my mental outlook. I need never feel old if I constantly rejuvenate myself by embracing only thoughts of my vitality and youth.

AFFIRMATION

**I am a beautiful reflection of the timelessness
of eternal life.**

Jewels for the Soul

253

*My jewel for
today is...*

DEDICATING EACH DAY TO GOD

Before rising from my bed each morning, it would serve me well to take a moment to dedicate the upcoming day to the service of the Mother-Father God. In Their presence and according to Their will, I shall step into my day and do all that is possible to bring Divine Light and Love to my corner of the world.

AFFIRMATION

***At the beginning of each new day I dedicate myself
to the service of love and light.***

Jewels for the Soul

*My jewel for
today is...*

SPONTANEITY

Life is meant to be lived with spontaneous zest and vigor. But being a spontaneous spirit is not always easy. Often, I need to remind myself to act with spontaneity. Physical life has conditioned me to think before I speak and look before I leap. When I seek oneness with the Infinite and open my heart to unconditional love, I need not fear the results of my spontaneity.

AFFIRMATION

**The spontaneous reactions of my spirit are always
loving and inspired.**

Jewels for the Soul

*My jewel for
today is...*

OVERCOMING INERTIA

God helps those who help themselves. I think I am being spiritual when I tell myself that if I wait patiently long enough, the Universe will resolve all my problems. This may be true. Still in all, there are many things that Spirit wants me to do to get the ball rolling in order to overcome my physical inertia and to signal Heaven that I am indeed seriously ready for action.

AFFIRMATION

The way of the Spiritual Warrior is to prayer for guidance, meditate to receive the answer, then take the initiative with integrity and full confidence.

Jewels for the Soul

My jewel for
today is...

BEING CENTERED IN HAPPINESS

If I center myself in happiness each day, I will be more likely to see the joy and pleasure being offered me through all people and situations I encounter. Being centered in happiness becomes a snap once I am ever mindful that my anchor in life is the bliss found in the power and the presence of the Living Spirit.

AFFIRMATION

When I anchor my soul in Spirit's love, my life
becomes centered in true happiness.

Jewels for the Soul

*My jewel for
today is...*

MY SPIRITUAL EDUCATION

When I first set out upon my spiritual journey in search of Divine Truth, I was taught to believe in that which I could not see. Now, I am learning to see that which is not visible. My spiritual education is a lifetime commitment. I must become comfortable with the fact that I am always at my beginning.

AFFIRMATION

The more I learn, the more I realize that there is no end to my spiritual quest for Truth.

Jewels for the Soul

*My jewel for
today is...*

INTER-DIMENSIONAL LIVING

For all Children of Light, life is lived on more than one plane of existence or within more than one dimension. Life in the third dimension is very familiar and satisfying for most people. However, striving for at-one-ment with the Holy Spirit dictates that I reach continually for higher levels of Infinite Reality. As I increase my level of awareness I quickly move into higher dimensions of being.

AFFIRMATION

Inter-dimensional awareness grants me a more holistic perspective of the supreme meaning and mystery of life.

Jewels for the Soul

*My jewel for
today is...*

MAKING CHECKLISTS

A sense of order and accomplishment are essential to the maintenance of physical and spiritual self-esteem. Making checklists is a wonderful way for me to bring order into my daily life. First, I shall list all of those things I need to do. Then I shall list all the things I want to do. By combining the two lists, I can easily compile one list of all that is realistically possible for me to do, ending my day with an invigorating sense of accomplishment.

AFFIRMATION

**Through the benefit of checklists, Divine Order
is created in my life.**

Jewels for the Soul

*My jewel for
today is...*

GRACEFUL BODY MOVEMENT

Graceful, fluid movements of the body are an excellent way to keep the flow of vital energy on track. In yoga or dance class, I can strengthen my spine, stamina, and sense of serenity, through controlled, elegant body movements. I need to remember my physical body is an extension of my spiritual body. Becoming physically attuned to the sway and undulations of the Universe affords deeper insight into the Cosmic Dance of Ecstasy.

AFFIRMATION

**The beauty and splendor of the Goddess is
witnessed in the graceful movements
of the human body.**

Jewels for the Soul

*My jewel for
today is...*

KEEPING MY EYES ON HEAVEN

Holy Spirit, there is so much to deal with in the world today. There is suffering, there is ignorance, and there is lack of faith. I do my best to stay centered, loving, and focused on Spirit. Yet, I ask Your help to strengthen my resolve and to lift my, sometimes, heavy heart. In all that I do let me do it for You, while keeping my eyes fixed on Heaven.

AFFIRMATION

*I easily fulfill my mission on Earth by keeping my
consciousness focused on the Will of Heaven.*

Jewels for the Soul

*My jewel for
today is...*

LOVING TRANSFORMATION

There is nothing on Earth or within my private life
that I can change by hating it. Love is the only power
for positive change. For love is the power of God.
If I want to know true peace in my time, then first I
must love peace into being. If I desire to know the
ecstasy of Divine Love, then first I must give love
away. All global and personal transformations must
be precipitated by the power and presence of love.

AFFIRMATION

**The essence of my being and the seed of all
transformation is love.**

Jewels for the Soul

*My jewel for
today is...*

EMBRACING MY TOTALITY

As I journey through this land of illusion, it is my task to remain ever mindful of embracing my totality. Because I am a Light Being, I cannot ignore the needs and desires of my physical mind and body. Though I am clad in human armor, I dare not forget my allegiance to my eternal reality as one with Spirit. Remaining conscious of my connection to both Heaven and Earth is my key to enlightenment.

AFFIRMATION

**Today, I embrace my totality and am made
whole by celebrating all aspects of
myself as Spirit in form.**

Jewels for the Soul

My jewel for
today is...

EXPERIENCING TRUTH

Great Spirit does not want me to live my life on blind faith. In fact, Spirit commands that I challenge it by asking for what I want, believing in my heart it is already mine. As I witness the manifestation of my dreams, I am given great reason to have a working faith founded in the powers of The Infinite. Universal truth can only become my personal truth after I have put it to the test and experienced its reality for myself.

AFFIRMATION

My heart is purified and strengthened as I seek to
make eternal truth my personal reality.

Jewels for the Soul

*My jewel for
today is...*

PERSONAL ACHIEVEMENT

There is a voice within telling me to go for it. Now is the time for me to plant the seeds of my personal agenda. What do I want to achieve, just for me, this day? Where is it that I have always wanted to travel? Or what can I start saving for that which I have always wanted to have? I must remember, that a thousand mile journey begins with the first step.

AFFIRMATION

**My personal achievements reflect the level
of Divine Light that I have recognized
within myself.**

Jewels for the Soul

*My jewel for
today is...*

Anonymous Giving

Imagine how thrilling it would be to receive a gift of genuine love from an anonymous giver. A simple note of encouragement, or a heartfelt poem re-inforcing another's loveliness would surely bring unforgettable cheer to an otherwise ordinary day. Today, I shall think of an original way to brighten the day of someone I know, as I brighten my own day with the joy of anonymous giving.

Affirmation

***As I give of myself, without thought of
compensation, I receive in return,
beyond comprehension.***

Jewels for the Soul

*My jewel for
today is...*

ESSENTIAL PURITY

If I truly comprehend that within the Universe there is only One Loving Spirit, One Unlimited Source, dedicated to my happiness and well being, then why do I so often give way to worry? Worry is nothing more than doubt. Doubt is a direct lack of faith. Furthermore, over time, worry's personal vibration will erect a very tall wall between me and my highest good.

AFFIRMATION

**My personal vibration is increased manifold by
the purification of my thoughts
and actions.**

Jewels for the Soul

*My jewel for
today is...*

GLORIFYING MYSELF

At this moment, for better or worse, I am the sum total of everything I have ever thought, said, or done. Yet, above all else, I remain the image and glory of God. I live by the breath of the Goddess. I am the Spirit of Love. Any and all transgressions, over which I carry guilt, are nullified in the presence of Supreme Radiance. At any moment in time, I can dedicate my life to the glory of God/Goddess and I can begin again.

AFFIRMATION

**By revering the glory that is mine, I give glory
to the God and Goddess.**

Jewels for the Soul

269

*My jewel for
today is...*

CELESTIAL MOTHER

She is the Universal Feminine Principle. The
Celestial Mother is the Queen of Heaven and Earth.
Every ancient civilization has suckled life from her
breasts, and hailed Her Divine. Today, I will pay
homage to her likeness in all women. On this day,
I will take time to acknowledge the magnificent
contributions of all mothers to the survival,
nurturance, and upliftment of humankind.

AFFIRMATION

*I give thanks to the Celestial Mother for my life,
which is a gift of Her Divine Love.*

Jewels for the Soul

*My jewel for
today is...*

STABILIZING ENERGY

As a Light Bearer, I am also a healer. I have been beckoned to this realm to offer my unique brand of healing to Earth's inhabitants. One of the most important ways I help heal the planet is by stabilizing scattered or fluctuating energies. If I find myself in the presence of hostile or confused behavior, by refusing to be drawn in emotionally and concentrating mentally on a positive outcome, I can assist in stabilizing any negative or shifting energies.

AFFIRMATION

I can stabilize any unstable situation by holding a vision of its perfection in my mind.

Jewels for the Soul

271

*My jewel for
today is...*

TRANSCENDING PERSONALITIES

The Earth has often been referred to as the University of Life. Of all the courses offered here, the hardest to ace is, transcending personalities. Learning to go beyond the words and deeds of kindred spirits, straight into the soul and substance of their being can be most difficult. For many, lifetime after lifetime has been devoted to the mastering of this one lesson.

AFFIRMATION

***Life's true value is witnessed through the transforming
power of relationships and true relating can only
happen soul to soul.***

Jewels for the Soul

*My jewel for
today is...*

BLESSING AND RELEASING

I have witnessed many of my brothers and sisters around me having to go without. There are homeless on the streets and families waving signs claiming they will work for food. If these unfortunate lives touch mine, I must act. I will give any food or money I can, asking Spirit to bless their lives as I have been blessed. Once I give of my own resources, and pray for Divine intervention, I must release the problem into Spirit's hands.

AFFIRMATION

*When another's problems touch my life, Spirit asks
that I offer my support. I will raise my voice in
prayer and release all concern in order for Spirit's
love to flow unencumbered.*

Jewels for the Soul

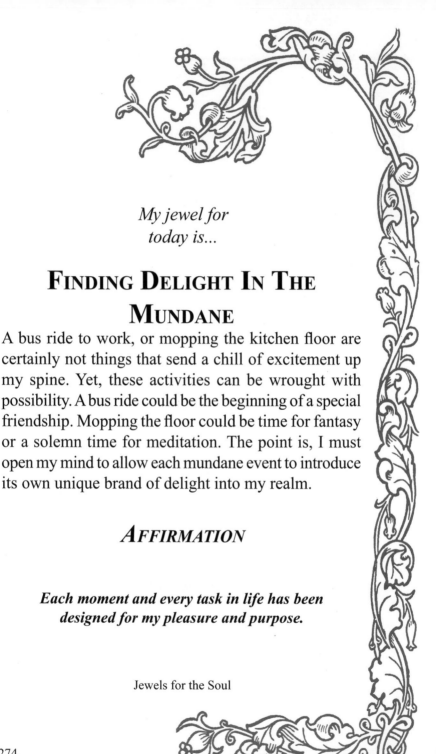

*My jewel for
today is...*

Finding Delight In The Mundane

A bus ride to work, or mopping the kitchen floor are certainly not things that send a chill of excitement up my spine. Yet, these activities can be wrought with possibility. A bus ride could be the beginning of a special friendship. Mopping the floor could be time for fantasy or a solemn time for meditation. The point is, I must open my mind to allow each mundane event to introduce its own unique brand of delight into my realm.

Affirmation

***Each moment and every task in life has been
designed for my pleasure and purpose.***

Jewels for the Soul

*My jewel for
today is...*

ALLOWING MY JOY TO SHINE FORTH

Joy is the natural state of Spirit. With eyes to see, it is obvious that every small child and creature alike, are intrinsically blessed with the Spirit of joy and happiness. Joy is my Divine Inheritance.

AFFIRMATION

***I will allow the joy of my being to shine forth as
a beacon of love for all to see.***

Jewels for the Soul

*My jewel for
today is...*

LOVING MY NEIGHBOR

The Beloved Master told us to, "Love thy neighbor as thyself." What better time to reach out and touch my neighbor. There are no mistakes in the Universe, so my neighbors were placed beside me for a reason. Today, I will introduce myself to a neighbor I've never met, or perhaps, I could invite my neighbor in for tea. Any sincere offer of love to my neighbor will make a huge contribution to the well-being of the entire planet.

AFFIRMATION

By initiating an atmosphere of friendship in my small neighborhood, I am shining the Light of Christ into every corner of the world.

Jewels for the Soul

*My jewel for
today is...*

RITUAL

The act of performing rituals, as a means of deeply penetrating and impressing the conscious and unconscious minds, has been employed by every great and powerful civilization. In my private world, performing rituals helps to focus my energies and brings a sense of spiritual tradition and order to my life. Whether I ritualize my morning coffee, or light candles beside my evening bath, these regular ceremonies are a form of worship.

AFFIRMATION

**By employing the art of ritual, I open my beingness
to the power of the Universal forces
within and around me.**

Jewels for the Soul

*My jewel for
today is...*

RECORDING MY DREAMS

Dreamtime is a sacred creation of Infinite Mind designed to convey the whispers of wisdom from the Great Spirit to the souls of Earth below. During dreamtime, I can receive inspired answers to lingering questions, and detailed descriptions of my future quest. Dreamtime demands my respect and offers me the greatest treasures of Heaven and Earth.

AFFIRMATION

*I will record my dreams and witness a picturesque
chronicle of my Higher Life evolve
before my very eyes.*

Jewels for the Soul

*My jewel for
today is...*

RELINQUISHING REGRET

Looking over my life, it is easy to recall many times when my behavior fell short of the spiritual ideal. I acted out of fear instead of faith, or I was grasping rather than trusting. There were also times when I sought to get even in lieu of reaching for understanding. But the point is, that I recognize my errors in judgment, and I relinquish the regret which will only impede my spiritual advancement.

AFFIRMATION

**In reality there are no right and wrong steps to
Spiritual Mastery, there is only
now and later.**

Jewels for the Soul

*My jewel for
today is...*

HEALING MY LIFE

Though illness may appear to invade my body, perfect health is my reality. At those times when I haven't got four quarters for a cup of coffee, my true supply is unlimited. When I see no light at the end of the tunnel, I am illuminated from within by the presence of the Holy Spirit. I can heal all appearances in my life by consciously acknowledging, on every level of my being, the presence and perfection of God.

AFFIRMATION

***I am instantly healed of all external effects by
shifting consciousness to the perfection of God.***

Jewels for the Soul

*My jewel for
today is...*

CARING FOR MOTHER EARTH

Mother Earth is the shelter of my body and soul. She gives Her energy so that I might share Her life. It is up to me to give in return so that we both can survive. By planting a garden of vegetables or flowers, I bring great happiness to the Earth and Her elementals. Simply buying and nurturing a new houseplant today, will contribute to the quality of life on this splendid orb.

AFFIRMATION

**I care for the Earth by respecting Her as a living
consciousness in need of loving attention.**

Jewels for the Soul

*My jewel for
today is...*

CAPTURING THE DAY

Today is unlike any day that has ever been or will ever be again. Today, I can choose to see with brand new eyes, or to don a great new attitude. It matters not what happened to me yesterday, and tomorrow is but a dream. Let me revel in the inherent joy of this moment in time while I savor the once in a lifetime deliciousness of being totally in the adventure of this day.

AFFIRMATION

Today will never come again, therefore, I shall open my heart to capture all the joy and wisdom it so lovingly longs to share.

Jewels for the Soul

*My jewel for
today is...*

WITHHOLDING OPINION

Because mine is a finite mind, I have not the capacity to understand the unlimited possibilities of energies at play in any given situation. What may present itself as a pretty cut and dried occurrence in the physical, may be infinitely more complex in the spiritual scheme of things. A mind cluttered with endless opinions has little room to grasp the true meaning of life.

AFFIRMATION

**I can appreciate the miracle of life when I learn
to withhold all opinions.**

Jewels for the Soul

*My jewel for
today is...*

IMAGINEERING

It is a metaphysical fact that my thoughts are energy forms that create my reality. Through the proper use of my thought forms I can perfect the art of imagineering. Any vision that I hold in my mind and accept as real will be made manifest in time. By holding the image of my future as bright and beautifully successful, I am actually commanding the cosmic forces of light and victory to do my bidding.

AFFIRMATION

***Through the power and practice of imagineering,
I will attract to myself all that I desire.***

Jewels for the Soul

*My jewel for
today is...*

KEEPING IN TOUCH

Dropping a quick note to a friend I haven't seen in a while, is an endearing way of telling them that they truly matter to me. Keeping in touch with short and long distance family, augments that blessed sense of belonging. Feelings of love and closeness are nurtured by simple and easy acts of reaching out with the intention of connecting with someone, heart to heart.

AFFIRMATION

*I encircle my life with a song of unending love
by keeping in touch with those near and
dear to my heart.*

Jewels for the Soul

*My jewel for
today is...*

ASSUMING PERSONAL
RESPONSIBILITY

The Mother-Father God has given me life, yet, I am co-creator with them. I am totally responsible for how I use or abuse my precious powers. The outer circumstances of my life are the fruits harvested from my inner visions. If I don't like something about my life, it is my responsibility to make the necessary changes in order to bring about the desired results.

AFFIRMATION

*I now assume sole responsibility for the conditions
in my life, knowing that I have the power to change
anything that no longer serves me.*

Jewels for the Soul

*My jewel for
today is...*

KNOWING SPIRIT

So many times in a single day, I become confused as to whether I am receiving messages from Spirit or from my ego mind. I feel that it is often impossible for me to know the difference, yet, as quickly as that thought passes another thought enters, saying, "Be still, and know that I AM." Spirit's identity is unmistakable. Spirit's power and presence are undeniable.

AFFIRMATION

*I will still my thinking mind and I will know, without a
doubt, when the voice of Spirit
sweetly whispers my name.*

Jewels for the Soul

My jewel for
today is...

PROJECTING MY POWER

I was conceived in the image of God. Like The Infinite, I am powerful. Like the Universe, I am unlimited. I came to Earth to use my powers for good. I have come to display my likeness to God. Hiding my light under the proverbial bushel, glorifies no one. To hide my likeness of love and light is indeed an insult against the Holy Spirit.

AFFIRMATION

I project my power into the world so that it may multiply, touching the lives of many.

Jewels for the Soul

*My jewel for
today is...*

SELF-ACCEPTANCE

No one is as critical of me as I am of myself. Of course, no one spends as much time looking for my faults, as I do. Deep in my heart, I know that I am exactly the way I was intended to be. If my arms are a little long, that's okay, for I can give a better hug. If I am a little short, so be it, for I get to stand closer to the hearts of others.

AFFIRMATION

**My heart center bursts with unconditional love for
the world, as I learn to accept myself,
exactly as I am.**

Jewels for the Soul

My jewel for
today is...

SEEKING TRUE LOVE

Every single one of us on Earth today, longs to know *true love*. Unfortunately, there are as many definitions for the meaning of *true love* as there are people seeking to find it. True love can only be found in my holy relationship to the Indwelling God. For this is the purest, simplest, and most enduring power in the Universe. True love of God and self is the only love worth seeking, for once I find it, all other treasures of the Heavenly Kingdom lie within my reach.

AFFIRMATION

Once my heart has been touched by the ecstasy
of Holy Love, true love in physical
form will find me.

Jewels for the Soul

*My jewel for
today is...*

STUDYING NATURE

Hermes said, "As above so below, as below so above." Quite simply, he is telling us that every major cosmic drama is played out in miniature here on Earth. By studying the spontaneous unfoldment of life in nature, I can observe the eternal wisdom of the cosmos. Long before the advent of books and weekend seminars, the Wise Ones relied on the life of nature to reveal the mysteries of life within the human soul.

AFFIRMATION

**The key to self-understanding can be found in
the study of the rhythm and cycles of nature.**

Jewels for the Soul

*My jewel for
today is...*

RETREAT

Despite all my efforts to remain positive and protected from outside negativity, there are times when I simply feel a tremendous need to be totally alone. Solitude is often the only means of recentering my scattered self. With special attention to diet, meditation, and relaxation, I emerge from my retreat recharged and able to love more fully from an open heart.

AFFIRMATION

**I enter the Kingdom of Heaven when I
retreat in solitude.**

Jewels for the Soul

*My jewel for
today is...*

SLOWING DOWN

Too often, I find myself rushing about, thinking only of my destination without taking time to enjoy the journey. To be in the now means that I seize the uniqueness of this very instant, without giving thought to where I have just been or where I need to be shortly. By slowing down enough to experience the sights and smells around me, my mind is more anchored in the present. By remembering to breathe deeply, my being is firmly connected to the moment.

AFFIRMATION

**Slowing down my physical pace gives my senses a
chance to absorb the resplendent joy found in
living one moment at a time.**

Jewels for the Soul

*My jewel for
today is...*

EXPECTANCY

As I learn to trust the loving energy of Spirit, I cease to struggle with the ups and downs of physical life. As challenges arise in life, I simply turn within, always expecting Spirit to provide me, unfailingly, with the enlightened guidance I need most.

AFFIRMATION

***By living in a state of perpetual expectancy,
I prepare myself to receive spiritual
illumination whenever I need it.***

Jewels for the Soul

*My jewel for
today is...*

AROMATHERAPY

It has been concluded in scientific circles, that the sense of smell is the strongest sensory trigger of memory, in this and perhaps even past lives. The essential aroma of certain plants and flowers have either a calming or stimulating affect on the human nervous system. Because the sense of smell is so consequential, it behooves me to educate myself regarding the ancient art of aromatherapy.

AFFIRMATION

Yin and Yang are balanced by the plants and flowers in Spirit's garden.

Jewels for the Soul

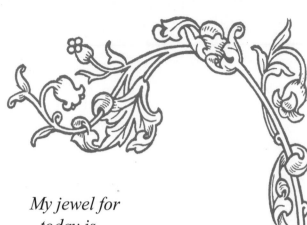

*My jewel for
today is...*

FENG SHUI

The ancient Chinese invented the art of Feng Shui over four thousand years ago. It was known as the Art of Placement. To know the right spot and proper direction to place one's house, was to create a flow of chi that guaranteed a lifetime of luck and prosperity. Today, Feng Shui remains a gift of divine understanding. As we embrace our living space as sacred, we manifest within our homes the tranquility of Heaven on Earth.

AFFIRMATION

**I open my life to natural serenity with the
study of Feng Shui.**

Jewels for the Soul

*My jewel for
today is...*

EXTRATERRESTRIAL REALITY

We are not alone in the Universe. We have been visited by our intergalactic family since long before recorded history. Expanding my consciousness to include the reality of my extended family is the next practical step in my personal evolution.

AFFIRMATION

**There is but one Spirit. I extend my love to its
every creation, both here and on
distant planets.**

Jewels for the Soul

ABOUT THE AUTHOR

Kathryn Peters Brinkley is an author, journalist, lecturer, metaphysica minister, Reiki Master, and certified Holistic Health Therapist who ha been dedicated to excellence in her work while driven by an insatiabl thirst to understand the eternal truths of the Universe. For as long as sh can remember, Kathryn has found herself attuned to the higher frequencie and dimensions. She became aware of her Angelic Guardians when the made themselves visible to her at the age of four. In a visitation from th Archangel Uriel, Kathryn was told the secret to the purpose of her life. A that time her Angels infused her with the knowing that she was on Earth t "uplift the hearts of man." Through their powerful and protective presenc Kathryn deepened her understanding of life's mysteries as she lived t face a myriad of life challenges, including the tumultuous aftermath o two life altering near-death-experience.

This unveiling of her unique calling caused Kathryn to explore th theosophies of different religions and spiritual practices from aroun the world. Her personal quest for spiritual understanding led Kathryn t first study the art of Astrology. Many answers to the Great Mysteries o Life were revealed to her through gaining this attunement to the Will o Heaven.

Once having achieved a substantial degree of personal wholeness an spiritual balance, she was divinely guided to open herself to assist other who were also seeking the Light of Spirit. Kathryn believes that we ar all capable of enriching our lives and becoming successful, fulfille human beings if only we allow the Divine Presence within to manifest i our daily lives. Health, happiness and prosperity are ours for the askin if we understand our ability to create them through the conscious use o Love.

True to her divine purpose, Kathryn offers **Jewels for the Soul** to uplif our hearts and help us to remember our Divine nature.

HeartLight Productions
1000 N. Green Valley Pkwy. Suite 440-292
Henderson, NV 89074-6170